THE HIGHEST TREE

THE HIGHEST TREE

The
Highest
Tree

A play by

Dore Schary

RANDOM HOUSE

NEW YORK

Photographs by courtesy of Friedman-Abeles

Library of Congress Catalog Card Number: 60–8374

Manufactured in the United States of America

To the memory of my mother, Belle Schary, who always told her children to try for the highest tree of human accomplishment, which, to her, was understanding and forbearance.

FOREWORD

In this poignant and absorbing play Dore Schary has succeeded in what I suppose is the aim of all drama—to portray a human situation in terms of characters so real that we care very much what happens to them. And if I remember my college courses, good drama also is so true, so universal, that knowingly or unknowingly we recognize ourselves in a kind of "there, but for the grace of God, go I." The timeliness of Mr. Schary's theme assures this feeling in *The Highest Tree*.

Aaron Cornish, the lovable and humane scientist, is confronted with the consequences of a human dilemma which is the dilemma of us all. And though we, like his family, still go unaware about our petty concerns, no one, I believe, who sees or reads this play will fail to understand how intimately the consequences of our oblivion may yet affect our lives and the lives of those who are to come after us.

We are told that the picture of contemporary English social conditions in the novels of Charles Dickens brought about great reforms of public policy in his time. Let us hope that this play—thoughtful, touching, amusing and delightful as it is—may prove to be just such a provocative work of art.

ADLAI STEVENSON

THE HIGHEST TREE *was first presented by The Theatre Guild and Dore Schary at the Longacre Theatre, New York City, on November 4, 1959, with the following cast:*
(*In order of appearance*)

AARON CORNISH	Kenneth MacKenna
ISABEL	Miriam Goldina
DR. ROBERT LEIGH	William Prince
SUSAN ASHE	Natalie Schafer
FREDERICK ASHE	Howard St. John
FREDERICK ASHE, JR. (Buzz)	Robert Redford
STEVEN CORNISH	Frank Milan
CALEB CORNISH	Richard Anderson
AMY CORNISH	Gloria Hoye
MARY MACREADY	Diana Douglas
BRONISLAUS PARTOS	Joe de Santis
JANE ASHE	Elizabeth Cole
ARKADY CLARK	Robert Ritterbusch
JOHN DEVEREAUX	Larry Gates
GLORIA CORNISH	Shirley Smith

Directed by Dore Schary
Settings and lighting designed by Donald Oenslager
Costumes by Marvin Reiss
Production manager, Jean Barrere
Associate producer, Walter Reilly

The home of Dr. Aaron Cornish
in the East Sixties, New York City.

ACT ONE

Two days before Thanksgiving. Early evening.

ACT TWO

SCENE 1. Late afternoon. The next day.
SCENE 2. An hour later.

ACT THREE

SCENE 1. Later that night.
SCENE 2. The next morning. Thanksgiving Day.

ACT ONE

Scene: The home of AARON CORNISH, *a brownstone house in the mid-Sixties, East Side, New York City. The house, built in 1891, retains a touch of the past with overtones of the present. It is furnished in quiet good taste.*

Of the first floor can be seen the living room, stage right, and the entrance hall, stage left. In the upstage wall of the hall is the door leading from the vestibule; and beyond that can be glimpsed the outer door and the street outside. Upstage left in the hall is a door leading into the library and the rest of the first floor of the house. Through it can be seen a love seat just below a street window with curtains and drapes.

Downstage left is a flight of stairs which leads, in view, to the second and third floors of the house.

Between the library door and the stairs, and off a landing elevated two steps, is a door leading downstairs to the kitchen.

Downstage right in the living room is a fireplace. Book shelves cover the upstage right wall. Two very tall windows, dressed in curtains and gold drapes, are in the upstage wall, left and right. Between the windows is a large circular pouf with a center pedestal on which rests a large vase of autumn leaves. On the wall above the pouf and between the windows hangs a painting of an edge of a wooded area featuring one tree higher than the others. Upstage left is a secretary and chair and, below it, a small portable bar.

Downstage right, below the fireplace, is an occasional chair with arms. Stage right there is a sofa and, in back of it, a long library table. Left of the sofa is a second occasional chair with

3

*arms and, between it and the sofa, a small table on which are
cigarettes, matches, and an ash tray. A third occasional chair
is in the arch, just below the bar, and a low ottoman is downstage left center to accentuate the division between the living
room and hall.*

*Downstage left, below the stairs, is a built-in bench and, left
of it, a table and lamp.*

*At a turn in the stairs, between the first and second floors,
stands a grandfather clock. Two doors open off the second floor
landing. The one upstage leads into the bedroom to be occupied
by* MARY MACREADY. *Through this door can be glimpsed two
windows with curtains and drapes and, between them, a dress-
ing table and a small chair.*

The door in the right wall of the landing leads into AARON's
*bedroom. It is furnished simply. Downstage right is a beige arm-
less occasional chair. Just above it, is an inlaid bureau. Up right
is a large, comfortable armchair. Two windows are in the upstage wall, left and right, and a large old and comfortable bed
stands between them. There are a small table right of the bed
and a reading stand left of it. Upstage left is a round table bearing the telephone, a lamp, books, and an ash tray.*

*At rise: It is Tuesday in late November, two days before
Thanksgiving, about five o'clock in the afternoon. The stage
is empty.* AARON CORNISH *enters the vestibule. He opens the inside door, using a key, and enters the hall. He is smoking a pipe
and carries an envelope-style zipper briefcase and a well-traveled
and worn suitcase. He closes the door, hangs his soft hat on the
rack right of the door, lays the briefcase on shelf by rack, and
crosses to set his suitcase just above the stairs. He then removes
his tweed topcoat, hangs it on the rack, picks up the briefcase
and moves into the living room, pausing above the small table
near the sofa to remove his pipe from his mouth and place it in
the ash tray. Then he continues right as* ISABEL, *having heard*

the door, enters from the kitchen. She is a strong-looking Spanish woman, about sixty years old.

ISABEL   Welcome home, Dr. Cornish!

AARON   How are you, Isabel?

ISABEL   Fine, thank you. It is good to see you—especially good! What time will Mr. Caleb and Amy be here?

AARON   They're due at seven o'clock.

ISABEL   I'll be so glad to see them.

AARON   So will I. Let's have dinner at seven-thirty.

ISABEL   Yes, Doctor. Oh, your sister, Mrs. Ashe, called. She said she will come by to see you before dinner.
(*The door buzzer sounds*)

AARON   Thank you.
(ISABEL *crosses into the hall and opens the door, admitting* DR. LEIGH, *a handsome man in his early forties*)

ISABEL   Good evening, Dr. Leigh.

LEIGH   Hello, Isabel. (*Without a pause, he places his black bag in the chair below the bar, removes and drops his coat over it, and goes to* AARON) Aaron.
(ISABEL *closes the door and hangs up* LEIGH's *coat*)

AARON   (*As they shake hands*)   Hello, Bob. How's Barbara?

LEIGH   Wonderful. She sends love.

5

(*A pause.* AARON *and* LEIGH *wait until* ISABEL *exits to the kitchen*)

AARON Have you spoken to Dr. Fitzhugh?

LEIGH Not yet. First I wanted to talk to you.

AARON For the past three days I've been on a treadmill—an endless belt of bewilderment and panic.

LEIGH I wanted to be with you.

AARON I know. I appreciate that. But there was no point. It's all there. (*He hands* LEIGH *the briefcase*) Every test—every single bit of medical testimony.

LEIGH (*Sitting on the sofa, and holding the briefcase*) Tell me about it, Aaron. I can see you want to talk.

AARON I have to. After I spoke to you last Wednesday, I checked into Bethesda for what was a routine checkup as far as the staff and the papers were concerned. They went over me—painstakingly—efficiently. The newest tests—the most precise examinations—by the best-informed specialist.

LEIGH Fitzhugh is the best.

AARON Yes. Well, I stayed there until yesterday morning. I had enough knowledge of what was happening to me, so that Fitzhugh had to tell me straight out. After that, I went to the office to tell Devereaux. He was at Canaveral. I left word for him to call Dr. Fitzhugh at Bethesda when he came in. Fitz will give him the details. I'm sure Devereaux will be quite upset (*Turning and taking a few steps*)—not nearly as much as I am. Then I called you. (LEIGH *nods and starts to open the case*) I believe you'll find the conclusions in that report incontrovertible.

LEIGH   Aaron—

AARON   Almost all my life I've dealt with the assumption that science lives in the field of suspended judgment. But this is incontrovertible.

LEIGH   I'll look at them. Then we'll talk.

AARON   Bob, my friend, what can you say? Will you be able to give it another name—another prognosis? Those charts are crystal clear. Acute leukemia. Prognosis: terminal.

LEIGH   Is that what they told you—or are you assuming it's so?

AARON   They told me. I insisted on knowing. I was quite brave about it then—but now I'm sick with fear. Waves of panic rush from my groin up to my skull. And I've been plotting— I've counted a dozen ways I can get out of this—quickly and painlessly—(*A wave to* LEIGH, *who looks worried*) I've no intention of doing any of them.

LEIGH   Your old Puritan stock.

AARON   Nonsense—I'll tell you why I've rejected them all. Because in this fine, well-oiled, orderly mind, I have the notion it won't happen to me. Yes—I think that perhaps I'll be that freak that fools the experts—that extra-special case history that's recorded in medical journals. Or, perhaps tomorrow— some inspired colleague will come up with a cure for what ails me. There's Aaron Cornish for you—behaving like any other foolish human who finds he's facing death.

LEIGH Why shouldn't you, Aaron—

AARON Because no one expects me to.

LEIGH (*Rising*) I'm afraid to talk, Aaron—not knowing what are the right words or wrong words to say to you.

AARON You're here. That's enough for now. Bob—at first I wanted to run far away—from everyone I know and love. But I've come home (*He sits in the chair near the sofa*)—not knowing how I'll be able to face any of them.

LEIGH You don't want any of them to know?

AARON No—not now. Only Caleb. I'll tell him. (*Suddenly weary and spent*) How does a father tell such a thing to his son?

LEIGH Can I spare you that?

AARON (*Shaking his head*) He'd want me to tell him. When you die suddenly, you face none of the people you love. You're gone—kaput! But in these instances, you have to face the fading away. (*Rising*) There's Caleb, Amy—and my sister, and my brother, Steven. And dear, darling Mary Macready—what can I say to her?

LEIGH Is she still in Italy?

AARON She's due in Washington tomorrow. She wanted to be with me for Thanksgiving. I've invited her here.

LEIGH   Ask me for any help I can give.

AARON   What I need is the composure to face all of the things that are so real—and now seem so unreal. I'll need your ears, Bob. I haven't any others to talk to. (*The phone rings.* AARON *crosses into the hall to answer it.* LEIGH *is near the sofa, unzipping the case and looking at the charts during the call*) Hello. . . . Yes, this is Aaron Cornish. . . . Hello, Devereaux? . . . Yes. Frankly, I'd rather not discuss it on the telephone. You've talked to Fitzhugh, haven't you? . . . Then there's really nothing to be said. . . . When will you be here? . . . Fine. See you tomorrow. . . . Yes, I'll be expecting you. Goodbye. (*He hangs up and comes back into the living room*) As anticipated, he's upset. He's had this happen before. It complicates his sense of orderliness. But Devereaux's a good administrator. When one soldier falls, he has another standing by to take over. He probably has my replacement already selected.

LEIGH   When I met him, he reminded me of a sharp razor.

AARON   A sharp razor—on the working end of a bulldozer. He's coming here tomorrow. (*The door buzzer sounds*) Bob—your word! You're not to tell anyone!

LEIGH   My word.
        (ISABEL *has appeared and answers the door, admitting* SUSAN *and* FREDERICK ASHE. SUSAN *is one year older than* AARON, *well groomed, efficient and able. Her husband,* FREDERICK ASHE, *is a lawyer in his fifties, stocky and straightforward in his manner.* ISABEL *takes* FRED'S *coat and hangs it up as* SUSAN, *still wearing her hat, gloves and fur coat, crosses to meet* AARON *just inside the living room*)

9

SUSAN   Aaron, darling! (*They embrace*) You look rested. I'm glad.

AARON   You look tired. I'm sad.

SUSAN (*To* LEIGH)   Hello, Bob.

LEIGH   Hello, Susan.
(*She goes back into the hall to be helped by* ISABEL *with her coat as* FRED *crosses below her into the living room*)

AARON   Good to see you, Fred!

FRED (*As they shake hands*)   Hello, Aaron. You look well! Real well!

LEIGH   Hello, Fred.

FRED (*Going to* LEIGH)   Hello, you old horse doctor.
(SUSAN *steps into the living room as* ISABEL *exits into the kitchen*)

SUSAN   Aaron, do they call off experimenting on Thanksgiving or is it always a happy coincidence that you're able to get home?

AARON   No, even physicists look forward to turkey. It's a pleasant contact with the certainties. Two wings, two drumsticks—everything as it always is.
(*He crosses to the fireplace*)

FRED (*To* LEIGH)   I'm pleased to see you, you faker. I've got a few questions.

LEIGH   Fire away. I'll hardly be listening
(SUSAN *crosses to sit on the sofa*)

FRED   It's about my leg. Damn thing's killing me. What's the funny name you gave it?

LEIGH   Meralgia paraesthetica—probably due in some way to your old broken-down disc.

FRED   It hurts a hell of a lot.
(AARON *sits in a chair*)

LEIGH   We could sever the nerve, but you'd hate the numbness almost as much as the pain. Relax, Fred. Learn to live with it.

FRED   Ooooh, that's the big new trend in modern medicine. "Learn to live with it." That's a fine profession. We lawyers ought to try that. A client comes in—he's in trouble—tax evasion— breach of contract—personal liability suit. We listen —nod wisely and say, "Learn to live with it. (*He extends a hand, palm up*) Twenty dollars, please. Next client!"

LEIGH   House calls these days are twenty-five dollars.

SUSAN   And you never do any of the things Bob tells you to do.

LEIGH   You see? I'm worth every cent you pay me.

FRED   Why don't I ever get a simple one-shot-and-it's-over sickness? Me, I always have to get something chronic.
(*He sits on the ottoman*)

SUSAN   Bob, how's Steven?

LEIGH Steven, at sixty-one, has the appetites of a twenty-year-old. That's how he is and that's what's the matter with his liver.

FRED Bob, you haven't answered my question. Isn't there something I should take for this leg?

LEIGH We have a brand-new medicine for it—aspirin. (*He extends his palm*) Twenty dollars, please. (ISABEL *enters from kitchen with an ice bucket.* LEIGH *takes it from her*) Thank you, Isabel.
  (*During the following, he sets bucket on the bar, fixes himself a drink and crosses back to the library table and the briefcase*)

SUSAN Isabel, are there other things you need for Thanksgiving? Any shopping I can do for you?

ISABEL No, thank you, Mrs. Ashe. I'll have everything just the way Dr. Cornish likes it.

SUSAN If you need extra silver or glasses, I can send them over from my home.

ISABEL We have all we need, thank you, Mrs. Ashe.

SUSAN But I will send some champagne—as a gift to my brother.
  (ISABEL *starts to the kitchen*)

AARON Thank you. Isabel, my friend (ISABEL *stops*)—keep the dinner under control. Don't extend yourself—simply as good as it always is.

ISABEL *Si me dejan tranquila, lo haré más facilmente y mejor.*

AARON *Paciencia,* Isabel.
(*She goes into the kitchen, closing the door*)

SUSAN Whenever she speaks Spanish, I know she is saying something perfectly dreadful about me.

AARON (*Edgy*) No. She merely suggests that she'd rather do things by herself.

SUSAN She's a beast about her kitchen. She always makes me feel like an intruder.

AARON To her, you are.

SUSAN Aaron!

AARON (*Rising*) Not to me, but to her. When Carla and I were married, Isabel came along as sort of a dowry—with a pledge to serve us both. Now, with Carla gone, Isabel dotes on protecting me from all imaginary problems.

SUSAN For heaven's sake, like what?

AARON Like family Thanksgiving dinners.

SUSAN You seem on edge, Aaron.

AARON I'm a little weary.

SUSAN Where were you these past few weeks, Aaron?

AARON Ohhh, I made a tour of some of the labs. Nothing exciting—just wearing.

FRED How goes the missile program?

AARON I have little contact with it, Fred.

FRED (*Rising and crossing to sit in the chair near the sofa*)
Really, Aaron, I can't understand what's going on. The
Russians keep beating us at everything. They not only *hit*
the moon—now they've got it *surrounded*. It's all their baby.

AARON Not really. Hopefully we'll catch up.

FRED We keep spending a fortune each year—billions—and yet
we keep falling behind. What's happened to our will to win?
Just because somebody else is out in front, you don't roll over
and play dead.

AARON (*Turning away*) No, you don't.

SUSAN Fred, you know Aaron doesn't like to talk about his
work.

LEIGH Will you all excuse me for a few minutes? I have some
calls to make.
(*As* SUSAN *nods, he takes the briefcase, crosses to the hall,
picks up the telephone and carries it into the library,
closing the door behind him*)

SUSAN Aaron, we'll be eleven for Thanksgiving dinner. We
four Ashes, Bob and Barbara, you, Caleb and Amy, and our
Jane is bringing a friend—a poet she says—and Steven alone
makes eleven.

AARON What about Gloria?

SUSAN   She detests me as much as I detest her.

AARON   She's Steven's wife.

SUSAN   Aaron, I was friendly to Steven's first three wives. The younger they get, the more I dislike them.

AARON   I'll ask her. And Mary Macready will be here.

SUSAN   That makes thirteen.

AARON   Are you superstitious?

SUSAN   No. I like Mary Macready—

AARON   "But you're old enough to be her father."

SUSAN   Aaron, you've been a widower for fifteen years. You've certainly a right to do whatever it is you wish to do.

AARON   (*Sharply*)   Certainly.

FRED   When's Junior due here?

SUSAN   Buzz said he'd be here about five-thirty.

FRED   Aaron, before he gets here, Susan and I want to talk to you about Junior.

AARON   Still calling him Junior? He's twenty-three and hates the name.

FRED   All right then—Buzz. *Buzz*. That's a name for a saw.

AARON   It's better than Junior.

SUSAN   We have a problem with him.

FRED   A damn serious one.

AARON   I don't know that *I* can help—

SUSAN   He's so fond of you, Aaron, I know he'll listen to you. We hate to burden you with this, but we've no one else to talk to. Steven is certainly no help.

FRED   As a matter of fact, I think that's part of the problem. When Junior came back from the Air Force, I had plans for him. All the plans a father plans. I wanted him to go back to college, take the bar, and come into my office. But no—he doesn't want any of that. He winds up a liquor salesman for Steven Cornish.

SUSAN   Fred, I think that—

FRED   (*Rising angrily*)   And don't tell me that Steve's shops are "food shops for the fastidious"! They're nothing but high-class saloons!

AARON   That's a harsh definition, Fred!

FRED   I like to be realistic.

AARON   Then why can't you see that your problems with Buzz aren't due to Steven or the Air Force. Not all sons want to be like their fathers.

FRED   Look at your son. Don't tell me you're not happy Caleb is teaching—starting the same way you did.

AARON Of course, I'm pleased about that. But he made that decision for himself.

SUSAN The problem, Aaron, is that Buzz wants to get married.

AARON Well, most healthy normal young men get around to that decision.

FRED But, Aaron, he's only twenty-three, and he's only earning seventy-five dollars a week!

AARON Oh, come, Fred! You'd be amazed at the number of young people living on that amount of money each week.

SUSAN Aaron, it isn't the money problem. Certainly Fred and I would be glad to help him—

AARON That's exactly what he wouldn't want!

SUSAN It's simply that the girl isn't the kind of girl we thought of for Buzz.

AARON What's wrong with her?

SUSAN Well—nothing. It's—we don't know her family. (AARON *turns away*) She seems like a simple—nice enough girl, but— Aaron, you're making this very difficult. I feel uncomfortable talking to you about it.

AARON Perhaps that's not my fault, Susan. You know you're very possessive. I have a feeling that you'd view any girl who came into Buzz's life with some alarm.

SUSAN   Aaron, don't go Freudian on me, please.

AARON   I'm not. I'm suggesting that you're too possessive.

SUSAN *(Rising)*   Aaron, is it wrong for me to love my children or my husband or my brothers? Is it wrong for me to feel deeply about those things that matter? *(She looks to* FRED*)* Is it a sin to want to see them happy?

AARON   No, but there comes a time when a young man has to make his own decisions and, right or wrong, you've got to let him make them.

FRED *(Moving to* SUSAN *and putting his arm about her waist)* We're all for his getting married—at the right time—to the right girl.

AARON   Please forgive me, Susan and Fred, but what in the world can *I* do about it? I don't know the girl, and I happen to think that Buzz is capable of making up his own mind!

FRED   I keep thinking that Steven got married for the first time when he was twenty-three.

AARON   Buzz isn't Steven.

FRED   Well, Steven hasn't done such a good job with his own life and I don't like having him advise my son. He's been weaning him away from me—*(The door buzzer sounds;* SUSAN *goes to answer it)*—simply because he believes the boy has no feeling for me.

SUSAN *(Almost at the door)*   Please, Fred—

AARON   That's damned silly, Fred! It doesn't become you.
(FRED *sits down.* SUSAN *opens the door to admit* FREDERICK
ASHE, JR., *a stalwart young man of twenty-three. He
kisses her*)

SUSAN   Hello, Buzz, dear.

FREDERICK, JR.   Mother, you look stunning as usual!

SUSAN *(Pointedly)*   Father's here.
(FREDERICK, JR., *slips off his coat, places it across the chair
below the bar and moves toward the center of the room*)

FREDERICK, JR.   Hello, Dad.
(*He touches* FRED's *shoulder in passing*)

FRED   Hi, son.

FREDERICK, JR.   Uncle Aaron—very glad to see you.

AARON *(As they shake hands)*   And I'm glad to see you, Buzz.
Want a drink?

FREDERICK, JR.   No, thanks. I can only stay a few minutes. Anyway, I hate the stuff. I only sell it.

FRED   Where you off to?
(AARON *sits at one end of the sofa*)

FREDERICK, JR.   I have a date for dinner.

FRED   When are we going to have the pleasure of your company
for dinner?

SUSAN (*Placatingly*) Buzz was with us last Thursday.

FREDERICK, JR. How goes it, Uncle Aaron? Are things as snafued as we're led to believe?
(*He sits at the other end of the sofa*)

AARON Not really.

FREDERICK, JR. (*Ducking his head as* SUSAN *strokes his hair*) I read a story in the paper this morning about some commercial jet that was examined for radioactive fallout. Is that on the level?

AARON Very much. When you explode hydrogen and atom bombs, the debris goes somewhere. (*He points up*) There's a good deal bobbing around—and it'll be there for years.

SUSAN Then you are against resuming the tests, Aaron?

FRED Why shouldn't we resume? The Russians certainly will.

AARON Yes, they will—if we do. And we will, if they do. It's a puzzlement, isn't it?

SUSAN Well, I think there's far too much talk about it. I think we should let all the people who know all about it make the decisions.

AARON Oh, darling, how right you are! Now, if you can get your hands on *all* those people who know *all* about it, you're on your way to Oslo for the Nobel.

FRED Would you get me a drink, please, Junior? (FREDERICK, JR., *gives him an angry look as he hears "Junior"*) Buzz?
(FREDERICK, JR., *goes to the bar and mixes a drink*)

SUSAN (*To relieve the moment of tension*) Are you going to stay home for a while, Aaron?

AARON Well—the fact is, I've felt for some time the need for a rest, travel—some reading—so I may be taking some time off.

SUSAN Are you going abroad?

AARON I'm not certain.

FRED Secret assignment?
(FREDERICK, JR., *brings the drink and gives it to* FRED. *Then he sits on the ottoman*)

AARON No. That's the strange life of a physicist. A normal vacation suddenly appears to be a secret assignment.

SUSAN Well, it was when you went to Los Alamos.
(*She sits on an arm of* FRED's *chair*)

AARON You have a stubborn memory. (*He rises, wanting to change the subject*) There's something else. Caleb is going to be in Chicago for years, and I rattle around in this house by myself and it's a drain. What if I were to try and sell it?

SUSAN (*Rising*) No, Aaron! Certainly not!

FRED Susan, it's Aaron's house. It's his to sell.

SUSAN It's been ours—the family's—for sixty years!

AARON But it's laminated with years and paint—and the memories belong to us whether we're here or not.

FRED Susan—your father left the house to your mother, and your mother left it to Aaron. I can remember the words: "I leave the family home and my little money to Aaron because Steven would waste it, Susan would hoard it, but Aaron will use it!"
(*After a second,* SUSAN *sits on the sofa*)

AARON And, Susan, the house is used up. We can't make a museum of it—"the Cornishes lived here." Who the hell are the Cornishes?
(*He turns away*)

SUSAN That's not funny.

AARON (*To her*) I started by saying I'd made no decision. I just want to think about it, that's all.

SUSAN (*Beginning her "soft sell"*) It's part of all of us—our children—

FRED Oh, nonsense. Aaron just told you that Caleb will probably be living in Chicago for years. Steven—well, he uses it occasionally as a bar or a motel—and, Susan, you have your own home—a little eight-room hideaway on Park Avenue.

SUSAN (*Gives him a look, then—*) Aaron, how could you say such a thing? "Who the hell are the Cornishes?" There were Mother and Father and Steven—and me—and our *children*—

FRED My children are named Ashe.

SUSAN (*To* FRED, *annoyed*) They're part Cornish! (*Back to* AARON) And there's you, Aaron. You're a famous man.

AARON   Susan, don't take on like this. Let's not talk about the house. I promise not to do anything about it until I discuss it with you. And I regret I insulted your family.

SUSAN   (*Rising and hugging him*)   Oh, Aaron, I love you. And I love Steven and I love all the things this house has meant. Do you understand?

AARON   Not really, but I believe you, and that's an end to it.

FREDERICK, JR.   Oh, Uncle Aaron, Mother has a great technique! Whenever she wants to win an argument, she talks quietly—real soft—and wins the day.

FRED   She doesn't win any arguments with you, Junior, and neither do I.
   (SUSAN *sits down again*)

FREDERICK, JR.   (*Rising and going to get his coat*)   I'm sorry, Uncle Aaron. I must leave. I have an appointment.

FRED   Who are you going out with tonight?

FREDERICK, JR.   (*Stepping toward his father*)   I have a date for dinner—with my girl.

FRED   You keep dropping in to say hello and then good-bye, and we never get a chance to really talk. Every damn night you're busy!

FREDERICK, JR.   Dad, please! ! !

FRED   (*Rising*)   For years you've been whoring around—

SUSAN (*Rising*) Fred!

FRED —now—suddenly—you're in love!

FREDERICK, JR. Dad, will you please shut up! ! !

FRED (*Grasping him by the upper arms*) You're always off for a date or a weekend or some other damn useless—Goddamit, Junior, you can't use our house as if it were some flea-bitten hotel where you can come and—

SUSAN Fred, please! Stop it!
    (FRED *releases* FREDERICK, JR., *and crosses to* SUSAN)

FREDERICK, JR. (*After a moment*) Sorry, Mother—Uncle. Good night.

AARON Buzz—

FREDERICK, JR. Let's talk about this some other time, please?

AARON (*Firmly*) I want you to stay. Can't you two find a way to talk to each other?

FRED (*Quietly, staring front*) Maybe there is a way. I haven't found it. Come on, Susan—(*He goes into the hall*) I've butchered Aaron's first hour at home.

SUSAN Fred—you know losing your temper is bad for you.

FRED (*Turning, rubbing his leg*) I know. And Junior is no tranquilizer.
    (*He goes to the rack and puts on his coat*)

24

SUSAN (*Goes up to* FREDERICK, JR.) Buzz, will you please see me when you get home?

FREDERICK, JR. All right, Mother.

SUSAN (*Moves toward the hall, pausing in arch*) I'm sorry, Aaron.

AARON It's all right. I'll see you tomorrow. You're coming for cocktails?

SUSAN Yes, we'll be here.
(*She goes to the rack for her coat and puts it on*)

FRED (*Crossing to* AARON—*quietly*) Good night, Aaron. Say so long to Bob.

AARON I will.
(FRED *turns, catching* FREDERICK JR.'s *eye. Father and son stare at each other, unable to bridge the chasm. Finally—*)

FREDERICK, JR. Good night, Dad.

FRED (*Nods*) 'Night.
(SUSAN *has opened the door.* FRED *follows her out.* AARON *moves to the sofa and sits down*)

FREDERICK, JR. Uncle Aaron—we all have a hell of a nerve—barging in on you and exploding all over the place.

AARON Families have a way of doing that. Tell me about your girl.

FREDERICK, JR. (*Quietly—still deeply disturbed by the scene with his father*) She's a secretary. I met her on a visit to a whole-

25

sale house. She's a year younger than I am. She's beautiful; her name is Anna, and I love her.

AARON   That's the full picture.

FREDERICK, JR.   I brought her over one Sunday for lunch and Mother and Dad looked her over as if she were an entry in a dog show.

AARON   Why don't they like her?

FREDERICK, JR. (*Sitting on the sofa—again in control*)   They didn't say. But I think they'd chalk off any girl right now. Dad's never gotten over my giving up the law. When I was thinking of staying in the Air Force, he kept saying I'd wind up as a drunken career soldier. Now he says I'll wind up as a drunken liquor salesman. Somewhere he's got the notion I'm going to wind up drunk, no matter what the hell I do.

AARON   Have you tried to talk to your folks about this matter quietly?

FREDERICK, JR.   Have I tried! Holy Toledo! I get up to "Listen Father," and Whamo!, he's all over me. Do you think you could talk to them? They'd listen to you.

AARON   They asked me to talk to you—said you'd listen to me.

FREDERICK, JR.   I will. Tell me. Anything.

AARON   You're sure you're in love?

FREDERICK, JR. (*Strongly*)   I'd die for her!

AARON You're in love. Can you support her?

FREDERICK, JR. Uncle Steve is raising me to one hundred dollars a week. He says in a year I'll be making one hundred fifty. And she works and makes eighty dollars. We can live just great on that.

AARON Yes, you can.

FREDERICK, JR. (*Rising and crossing*) Then why are they so against it? !

AARON Maybe they don't understand. Try telling them for once —quietly. For instance, what if they would listen to you— quietly—what would you say?

FREDERICK, JR. Okay. I'd say this, I think. Now listen, Father (*His anger builds throughout the speech*) —while working for Uncle Steve may not be the best job in the world, I like it fine. I've got ideas for the business and I'll make out just fine. I'm no boozer! I'd like to settle down, get married, raise a couple of kids! Now, what the hell—does that make me a failure? All right! If all this damn quarreling doesn't stop, I'm going to get out of the house and do what I damn please anyhow!

AARON I'd hardly call that a quiet talk.

FREDERICK, JR. Well, you see? There you are. Just thinking about him—I see him getting mad at me—and I flip my lid!

AARON This is small comfort to you, I know—but, Buzz, you're exactly like your father. (FREDERICK, JR., *looks at him incredu-*

lously) It's true. You look like him—talk like him, and lose your temper just as quickly.

FREDERICK, JR. (*Sitting down again*) I'll be damned.

AARON I don't think so.

FREDERICK, JR. (*After a brief pause*) Uncle Aaron, what I can't say to them is—that I want my own corner somewhere. I flew a jet plane and I'm not afraid of living or dying or anything. I want a place—a wife—a child—some place that will be mine. And even if a bomb falls—maybe there'll be something left— that was part of me. (AARON *looks away*) I guess that sounds foolish—

AARON (*After a moment*) No. Every one of us wants something left after we shuffle off—bombs or no bombs. (*He rises, moves away, and then turns*) Buzz, say all this to them—as you've said it to me. Try.

FREDERICK, JR. (*Rising*) Well—I've tried a hundred times—but you make it seem possible. I'll have a whack at it. If you hear a loud noise, that's Father blasting off. (LEIGH *returns from the library, carrying the briefcase and telephone. He places the latter on its shelf*) Oh, hi, Doctor.

LEIGH Hello, Buzz.

FREDERICK, JR. (*Turning back to* AARON, *after picking up his coat*) Say, Uncle Aaron—you weren't kidding about my being just like my—you-know-who?

AARON No, I wasn't.

FREDERICK, JR. That's the biggest shock I've had since I bailed out at ten thousand feet!
   (*He exits*)

LEIGH What was all that about?

AARON Problems of the living. The living have many problems.

LEIGH Aaron, I'd like to call Dr. Fitzhugh.

AARON I'll put in the call. You can take it upstairs—for privacy. I'll listen in down here.
   (LEIGH *nods, takes the briefcase upstairs.* AARON *goes to the light switches. He touches three switches, turning on lights in the hall, living room, and vestibule. He then goes to the telephone, picks it up, dials three numbers, waits a second, and then dials seven more. Meantime,* LEIGH *has entered* AARON's *bedroom and has turned on the light and closed the door. He takes the phone from the round table and carries it to the bed. He opens the briefcase, then picks up the phone*)

LEIGH Hello.

AARON Hello, Bob.

LEIGH Aaron, do you think it's necessary for you to listen to all this?

AARON No, but I'd prefer it.

LEIGH (*The Washington number has answered*) It's Dr. Robert Leigh of New York. I'd like to speak to Dr. Fitzhugh. Please tell him I'm Aaron Cornish's physician. Thank you.

29

AARON That'll get you action. (*He looks toward the library and the kitchen doors*) I'm taking the phone into the living room. I'll be right back. (*He disengages the phone from its jack and carries it into the living room and connects the jack near the fireplace wall. He sits on the sofa and picks up phone*) Hello, up there.

LEIGH Hello. (FITZHUGH *evidently answers in Washington*) How do you do, Dr. Fitzhugh.

AARON Hello, Fitz.

LEIGH Dr. Cornish is on the extension.
(*He sits on the bed and refers to the charts and X-rays that were in the briefcase*)

AARON Fitz, Bob Leigh has gone over the charts I brought in— but with the morbid curiosity of your peculiar profession, he is anxious to confirm.

LEIGH Doctor, I'm referring to the C.B.C., checking if I may, the figures with your copy. . . . Thank you. (*He reads*) Hemoglobin ten grams. R.B.C. three point three. W.B.C. fifteen thousand. Poly twenty. Lymph ten. Monocytes four. Myeloblasts sixty-six. Yes—platelets twenty thousand. Yes, I've seen the X-rays. I note they're negative—taken merely to determine there can be no exacerbation under medication. Yes—yes—metacorten daily twenty milligrams. I wanted to ask you about the use of S.M.P.

AARON What's that, Bob? None of your shorthand.

LEIGH Six-mercapto-purine.
(*They listen*)

AARON Thanks, Fitz. I'm glad I'll be spared that for a few weeks.

> (*He hangs up, rises and moves about, lost in thought, his back to the audience*)

LEIGH Aaron? . . . No, Doctor, he's been talking about it quite fully. . . . Yes, I'll suggest sedatives at night. . . . Oh, I agree. The C.B.C. certainly leaves no doubt of the type—it's myelo-blastic. (AARON *unplugs the phone, coils the cord, carries the phone back to its shelf in the hall and engages it in the jack there. He returns to the living room. Meantime*—) Yes, Dr. Fitzhugh, I'm stunned and sick about it. I know. . . . I'd like to be in touch with you at least once a week. . . . Yes, Doctor, I'll keep them with me. Good-bye.

> (LEIGH *hangs up, returns the telephone to the table, puts the material back in the briefcase, and leaves the bed-room—not closing the door. He goes downstairs*)

AARON Did you ask him how long?

LEIGH No. He could only have guessed.

AARON (*Moving to* LEIGH) What's your guess?

LEIGH Please, Aaron. I don't know.

AARON Six months?

LEIGH Maybe longer.

AARON But not much longer. (*Agitated as* LEIGH *does not answer*) Bob! I won't be able to talk about this to anyone else!

LEIGH Isn't there someone in the family who should be told?

AARON No, not yet. The only one who should know is Caleb.

LEIGH Not Susan?

AARON (*Shaking his head*) Nor Steven. They have other worries. Bob, I'm not as afraid of death as I am of dying. Do you understand? (LEIGH *knows no answer is required.* AARON *sits on the sofa*) I've always felt that most people are of the same mind. It's the uncertainty of dying—will it be burning, drowning, violent pain—wasting unconsciousness? These are the matters that frighten us. Perhaps that is why the aged die with composure. They know they've escaped the thousand and one torturous dyings—and they go quietly.

LEIGH (*Placing the briefcase on the table and sitting on the sofa*) Aaron, I can't help wondering how related your illness is to your exposure to radiation.

AARON I've asked myself that question—much as a tightrope walker who—falling into space—wonders if his occupation is responsible for his unhappy flight. But my reason tells me acute leukemia is not an occupational hazard—merely a risk of the times in which we live. (*He rises*) It's idiotic! I feel strong and vigorous. I find it hard to believe.

STEVEN (*Entering the hall from the vestibule*) Good evening—anybody!
> (*He is two years older than* AARON *and one year older than* SUSAN. *He is immaculately groomed, fashionable and elegant. His manner is cultivated and worldly—but only his manner. He replaces his key in his pocket, slips off his coat and bowler hat, hangs them on the rack, and crosses swiftly into the living room*)

AARON Hello, Steve.

LEIGH (*Exchanges a look with* AARON, *rises*) Well—the elder Cornish.

STEVEN Bob. Fancy seeing you here. (*He crosses to embrace* AARON) How's my kid brother?

AARON Spry.

LEIGH I didn't hear the buzzer. Did you jimmy the lock?

STEVEN I still carry the key Aaron gave me. Making a quiet entrance is often helpful.
   (*He goes to the bar*)

LEIGH (*Watches* STEVEN *and then sits down*) Scotch is not exactly a specific for a bad liver.

STEVEN (*Bringing his drink to the sofa*) I have abiding faith in you. I never think about my liver. I expect to be around for a *long* time. (*He picks up the briefcase—looks at* AARON *mock-seriously*) Top secret?

AARON (*Sitting on the sofa*) Top.

STEVEN (*Laying the briefcase on the table*) You look well, Aaron. That same preoccupied stare—but well. Did you have a long rest?

AARON No, but I have one in mind.

STEVEN Where will you be going?

AARON I don't know where I'm going, Steven.

33

STEVEN Maybe we could go together.

AARON (*With a wry smile*) I don't think I'd like that.

STEVEN Well—that's brotherly.

AARON (*Covering*) Oh—your pace is too fast for me. You lead a rugged life, Steve.

STEVEN Ah, Fred has been talking.

AARON Why Fred?

STEVEN Because Isabel is too discreet to mention my few nocturnal visits here while you're out of town. Sue refuses to believe it's so. Buzz wouldn't dare. So that leaves Fred.

LEIGH What about me?

STEVEN I'm your patient. You'd never break a trust.

AARON Actually Fred has some right. He's your brother-in-law.

STEVEN He's a bore.

AARON You may not like him, but he's no bore.

STEVEN Buzz has blood in his veins. Fred keeps treating him as though he were a teen-ager. That kid's been around—seen half the world—flown a jet plane—bailed out twice—walked away from a crash landing—*and* he's slept with girls in a dozen cities. He's a man!

AARON Your qualifications for manhood are quite demanding.

34

STEVEN You know what I mean. Fred is too stupid to understand.
(*He drinks*)

AARON (*Sharply*) You also make reckless use of the word stupid!

STEVEN Something's bothering my kid brother. What's the
matter, Aaron? Something go wrong in the lab? Another
quarrel with Devereaux?

LEIGH Steve, he's a bit bushed!

AARON (*Sharply—rising*) No—it's—
(*He stops*)

STEVEN What?

AARON Ooh, nothing. Except you're an aged, beautifully
groomed juvenile delinquent.

LEIGH With a lousy liver.

STEVEN Good! I'll have another drink!
(*He crosses to the bar, finishing his drink*)

LEIGH (*Rising*) Aaron, I have a hospital call to make. I can be
back in an hour.

AARON (*Taking the briefcase from the table and handing it to
LEIGH*) No, Bob. Caleb should be here soon. We can talk
tomorrow.
(LEIGH *starts out.* STEVEN *has turned from the bar in time
to see the briefcase*)

STEVEN   Selling your secrets to the enemy?

AARON   Bob's working with me on this one. We're getting a hell of a price from the Russians.

LEIGH (*Drops the briefcase on a chair and goes to get his coat.* AARON, *following, picks up the briefcase and the black bag*) 'Night, Steve.

STEVEN   Good night, good doctor.

LEIGH (*Putting on his coat—to* AARON)   I'll see you in the morning.
  (AARON *nods.* LEIGH *looks at him closely.* AARON *extends the briefcase*)

AARON   I'll see you. For sure.

LEIGH (*Taking the briefcase and the black bag*)   Good night.

AARON   Good night, Bob.
  (LEIGH *exits and* AARON *returns to the living room*)

STEVEN   Aaron, if you're really annoyed with me, I can give back the key to this house.

AARON (*Sitting in the chair near the sofa*)   Liquor makes you petulant. Sit down. How's Gloria?

STEVEN (*Sitting on the sofa*)   Fine.

AARON   You'll both be here for Thanksgiving dinner?

STEVEN   Hope to. Gloria and Sue don't get along too well.

AARON I'll help keep the peace.

STEVEN Gloria's only thirty-two. She thinks Sue endures her. Sue, you know, has that strong maternal urge. She has to be Mama or she doesn't play. (*A brief pause*) I'm happy with Gloria.

AARON Good.

STEVEN Aaron—tonight you seemed to be teasing me—on the level—criticizing me.

AARON Perhaps I was. Your standards are a bit odd—but I wasn't judging them. I was thinking that you do try to impose them on others—so that a simple code of good behavior becomes, to you, bourgeois—sentimental.

STEVEN (*Rising*) Don't turn away from me. You're my anchor. (*He sets his glass on the table*) I talk about you with pride—make people think we are closer than we really are—make a point of telling people you're my kid brother.

AARON I am.

STEVEN But always, when I'm with you, I feel that you're the older one. I've always felt that because of what you've accomplished.

AARON (*Trying to break* STEVEN's *mood*) You're too knowing to be jealous of your brother.

STEVEN Aaron—(*He sits down again*) I need your help. It's my daughter. She's been here in New York for the past few months.

AARON   I didn't know that.

STEVEN   Well, her mother wrote me about four months ago and asked me to send money for Elizabeth to come on from Atlanta. Said she wanted to be a model. I've seen her twice.

AARON   How is Elizabeth?

STEVEN   She's a tramp—a slut. I knew it the first time I saw her —after fifteen years. I remembered her as a sweet pink and white girl—and here she is (*He rises and takes a step*)—hard as a rock and a series of visits to bed written all over her face.

AARON   (*Rising*)   I'm sorry to hear that. Are you sure?

STEVEN   (*Looks at him*)   I'm sure. (*He picks up his glass and goes to the bar*) I wasn't going to tell you, Aaron. That's what all this is for (*He indicates the liquor*)—courage to drown the humiliation. (*He pours Scotch into his glass and walks toward the sofa, putting his hand on the back of the chair near it*) Aaron, I'm a wreck of a man. I know it. Failed at three other marriages—failing with this one. I keep looking for youth, thinking I'll find it—knowing that I'm getting older— ashamed—and then looking again for strange rooms with strange girls available for a hundred dollars a night. And now my daughter—taking care of men (*He sets his glass on the small table*)—maybe like me. I didn't ask her what she charges. (*He bows his head*) I wish right now that I'd die.

AARON   Steven, don't wish your life away!
          (*He turns away*)

STEVEN   Please don't tell anyone, Aaron. I haven't been much of a father—or a husband—but I can feel shame.

AARON I'll tell no one.

STEVEN You're good at keeping secrets. Aaron, what can I do about her? (AARON *does not respond*) She's my daughter!

AARON (*Turning—suddenly snapping*) Damn it, Steve, it's late for you to take on the obligations of fatherhood. Where were you when Elizabeth was growing and needing? Did a few checks to Atlanta pay off for everything she didn't get?

STEVEN (*Shaking his head*) No—no.

AARON Forgive me.
   (STEVEN *nods, adjusts his jacket and starts to button it. He stops, looking down at his attire*)

STEVEN Look at me. All dressed up in three-hundred-dollar suits. Some day I may make the list of the (*He is on the verge of tears*)—ten best-dressed men (*He suddenly presses his wrists against his abdomen*)—in America. How (*He bends over and sinks into the chair near the sofa*)—my belly hurts. I hurt, Aaron, all over.

AARON (*Crossing to him, putting his arm on* STEVEN's *shoulder*) Steven, do you want me to find Bob? Can I get you some coffee? Anything?

STEVEN (*Shaking his head, tears crowding his eyes*) Those are the little questions, with the little answers. Get me a doctor. Get me a Bromo—or a cup of coffee. No, Aaron—for Christ's sake—what happens to us and why do we let it happen?

AARON I don't know the equations. (*Suddenly desperate*) Oh, Steve, don't look to me for anything! All I can offer you is some patience—some sorrow—and affection.

STEVEN (*Quietly, grasping* AARON's *hand*) I'll take that. It's enough. Have I got anything you want?

AARON Only the same.

STEVEN (*Takes a handkerchief from his pocket. As he rises and crosses to the hall for his hat and coat—*) You're expecting Caleb. I'd better clear out.

AARON Tell Gloria to be sure to come with you Thursday. Tell her I insist.

STEVEN (*Putting on his coat and taking his hat*) I will. And give Caleb and Amy my love. (*He returns to just inside the arch, and puts on his hat*) Do you like the new bonnet? (AARON *nods.* STEVEN *reaches into his coat pocket, brings out the house key and holds it out*) I can keep the key? (AARON *smiles his yes*) Good night.
      (STEVEN *exits.* AARON *turns and takes a few steps, exhausted.* ISABEL *comes in from the kitchen*)

ISABEL Excuse me, Doctor—it's after seven. I better plan dinner for later.

AARON (*Sitting on the sofa*) That might be a good idea.

ISABEL Dr. Cornish, you don't look well.

AARON That's a relief. Everyone else has told me I look splendid.

ISABEL *Sólo el sirviente conoce a su amo.*

40

AARON (*With a smile*) Do you really believe that?

ISABEL In this case, I do believe that the servant knows the master better than anyone else. I've seen more of you than the rest of your family. Something is troubling you—something serious.

AARON (*Rising*) Only my work, Isabel. Your fine Spanish intuition is letting you down.
>(*The door to the vestibule bursts open and* CALEB, AARON's *son, enters—followed by his wife,* AMY. *They are a handsome young couple.* CALEB *carries two suitcases and* AMY *carries an extra coat, her hat, a handbag, and a briefcase*)

CALEB Hello! Anybody home?
>(*He places the suitcases at the foot of the stairs, in a position to be carried up*)

ISABEL (*Crossing to him*) It's Mr. Caleb!
>(AMY *sets down the briefcase by the coat rack and hurries to* AARON *in the living room. The ensuing conversations occur simultaneously*)

CALEB (*Taking* ISABEL's *hands*) Isabel, my love.

ISABEL Hello! Hello!

CALEB You're getting more beautiful every day!

AMY (*Embracing* AARON) Hello, Aaron!

AARON Amy!

AMY It's so good to be here!

AARON Wonderful to see you!
(CALEB *crosses to* AARON *as* AMY *goes into the hall*)

CALEB (*Shaking hands*) Father! It's good to see you!

AARON Son!

CALEB Be back in a minute.
(*He crosses to the suitcases at the foot of the stairs and starts up*)

AARON Good.

AMY (*Handing the extra coat to* ISABEL) Hello, Isabel!

ISABEL Good evening, Mrs. Cornish.

AMY (*Placing her hat and bag on the table in the hall*) Amy. How are you?

ISABEL Fine, thank you.
(AMY *removes her coat and hangs it on the rack.* ISABEL *closes the outer door, picks up the briefcase and follows* CALEB, *still carrying* AMY's *extra coat*)

AARON Amy, you wait here and tell me whether or not my son's been treating you well.
(AMY *removes her gloves and lays them on the table with her hat and bag*)

CALEB (*From the stairs*) Father, I haven't slugged her in over a week.
(AMY *goes into the living room*)

AARON Cold drink?

AMY Not now, thanks. Later.

AARON How was the flight?

AMY (*As they sit on the sofa*) Too slow. Every minute up there seems like an hour to me.

AARON My lecture in aerodynamics was of no comfort to you?

AMY Not a bit. Isn't that awful? I love trains.

AARON How are your parents?

AMY Well—Mother has accepted another chairmanship. Shouldn't it be chairwomanship?

AARON Of course it should.

AMY Well, anyway, she's got another one. And Father won a prize in a club golf tournament. He's been impossible. He views himself as the Ben Hogan of the department store business.
    (CALEB *has deposited the suitcases on the third floor and has returned, taking off his coat and hanging it on the hall rack. He goes into the living room*)

CALEB Go on, Amy. Now the woman's work begins. Unpack.
    (*He sits on the chair near the sofa*)

AMY (*Rising and walking to the stairs*) Aaron, your son treats me like a squaw. (*As she starts upstairs*) I'll be back for that drink. (*She continues to the third floor*)

43

CALEB (*Taking a slip of paper from his pocket*) Father, your efficient staff sent me a list of the shows to see—the theatres—addresses. It's good you weren't in Washington last week. They were occupied worrying about me. By the way, where were you?

(*He lays the slip of paper on the small table*)

AARON (*Inventing rapidly*) Ohh—I made a trip to Canaveral. There was trouble with some transistors—trigger devices on the heads. Not my field, you know, but Devereaux keeps asking for fresh minds. He doesn't realize that mine is far from fresh.

CALEB Come back to teaching. That's a freshener.

AARON It goes well?

CALEB I manage to stay a lecture or two ahead of the class. Sometimes they almost catch up. There's so damn much new material in the field. (*Leaning forward*) Did you read the last report?

AARON Yes; we discussed it last week. The fudge factors make it less than definitive.

CALEB There's enough fact to frighten anyone—even Devereaux.

AARON Devereaux doesn't frighten easily. He takes the view that you geneticists are alarmists.

CALEB (*Rising*) That's me, Father! I am considerably alarmed!

AARON He takes the calm, rational view. Automobiles and planes bring us thousands of deaths each year—casualties of the twentieth century.

CALEB That's some "rational." We're dealing here with genes—the life plasma.

AARON Well, his answer is—better to live with some mutative changes—than in a slave world.

CALEB That's Devereaux. What about you?

AARON (*Rising*) You know about me. I disagree with Devereaux about almost everything.

CALEB Father, those damn fruit flies depress me. In the lab we see changes from radiation that won't be lost for hundreds of generations. And if the strontium load gets heavier—

AARON Caleb, we really don't know how heavy it is or how much we can take.

CALEB Father, we do know that the rate of leukemia has increased three hundred percent since the first atom bomb fell.

AARON Yes, I know that.

CALEB And the rate will keep increasing—more people will die —and the cold political logic is paralyzing all of us. (*A brief pause*) And we're not doing enough about it. Sometimes I think what we are doing is freezing. I mean, like animals freeze in time of danger—like a possum or a deer or a wolf will freeze at the first sight of an enemy. I wonder—are we all doing this freezing?

45

AARON (*Decides to stop "freezing" and tell* CALEB *of his illness. Stepping towards him—*) Caleb—

CALEB (*Interrupting*) Father, I have a question to ask you.

AARON That sounds ominous.
(AMY *starts downstairs from the third floor*)

CALEB Not ominous—but important. (*Sitting on an arm of the sofa*) I've been asked to serve on a committee—a new committee dedicated to oppose the resumption of atom and hydrogen bomb testing. But I won't do it if it, in any way, proves to be an embarrassment to you.

AARON Caleb, you're your own man.

CALEB I am also your son. I'd like your approval.

AARON (*Turning away*) Let me think on it.

CALEB I have strong reasons for doing this, Father.

AARON (*Turning back to* CALEB) Then there's no need to ask my permission. It will be no embarrassment to me.

CALEB (*Rising*) Won't you ask what my reasons are?

AARON I know your reasons. I understand them. I respect them. I'm merely not oriented to working on committees for anything.

CALEB Forgive me, Father, but I think all of us are going to have to change our orientation on a lot of things.

46

THE HIGHEST TREE

AMY (*Crossing into the living room from the stairs*) I'm warning you both! No shop talk!
(*She sits on the sofa*)

CALEB (*Sitting*) As I told you, Father, she has the mind of a cretin.

AARON Caleb has the arrogance of the half-educated man. You poor girl—you're much too good for him.

AMY I know that, but it's too late.
(*She gives* CALEB *a "tell him" inclination of the head*)

CALEB (*Nods and rises*) And that, Father, brings us to an unusually provocative announcement. Dr. Aaron Cornish—you are about to add another honorary title to your long list of degrees—paternal grandfather. (AARON, *laughing, happy, surprised, sits and embraces* AMY) Well, I would like appropriate congratulations.

AARON You have them! Every one of them! Oh, I'm excited and pleased and happy!

AMY I hope Caleb isn't too early about it. We heard from the rabbit just yesterday.

AARON Actually, when should the baby be here?

CALEB Well, if the rabbit, the doctor and the two of us know what we're talking about—the baby's due in seven months, and you're going to walk the floor with me!

47

AARON (*Thoughtfully*) Seven months. (*He smiles to conceal his thoughts*) That'll be June.
(ISABEL *starts down from the third floor*)

AMY Or early July.

AARON Well, if I have nothing more important to do, I'll be there. It's wonderful! Wonderful!

CALEB Now, Father, if you have any news to top that, we're willing to listen.

AARON Not a chance. (ISABEL *is at the bottom of stairs.* AARON *rises and turns to her*) Isabel! Good news! Amy is going to have a baby.

CALEB Both of us!

ISABEL Oh, good! Good! (*She walks to* AMY *and takes her hands, kissing one as* AMY *rises*) Congratulations! Oh, Doctor, you must be so happy!

AARON I've never been as happy.

CALEB (*Puts an arm around* AMY) Let me add to your euphoria. Amy has agreed that this first one be named for a Cornish. So, if it's a girl, the name will be Carla. If a boy, Aaron Cornish the Second.

AARON Thank you, Amy—and you, Caleb. I'm grateful.

CALEB Now you know why I feel so strongly about that new committee, Father.

48

AARON I don't blame you. By all means, join.

CALEB Perhaps I can help make a safer world for Aaron
Cornish the Second.

AARON I hope with all my heart that you do.

Curtain

ACT TWO

Scene 1

Scene: It is the following day, late afternoon. The sun comes in faintly from the west and fades during the action of the scene.

At rise: MARY MACREADY *is walking from the hall into the living room. She places her purse and gloves on the library table above the sofa, removes her coat and places it on the pouf.* MARY *is a young woman, handsome, about thirty years old.*

As MARY *leaves the hall,* ISABEL *starts up the stairs, carrying* MARY'S *suitcase and an extra coat.* AARON, *in his bedroom, combs his hair, adjusts his tie and starts to put on his coat as* ISABEL *knocks on his closed bedroom door.*

AARON   Yes?

ISABEL   Miss Macready is here, Dr. Cornish.

AARON   Thank you. (*The door of* MARY'S *room is open and* ISABEL *enters with the suitcase and coat, closing the door behind her.* AARON *comes out of his room and hurries down the stairs.* MARY *hears him and turns. They embrace and kiss*) Mary, my dear Mary.

MARY   Dearest. (AARON *looks at her*) Any signs of deterioration?

AARON   Not a one.

53

MARY   I should look dreadful. Nine hours on a plane from Rome to New York (*She kisses him lightly*)—plane to Washington (*Another small kiss*)—and here I am, chasing after you the same day. Washington wasn't anything without you.

AARON   The young are tireless. It's depressing.

MARY   If it makes you feel better, I'm exhausted.

AARON   You look radiant.

MARY   I don't. My trip was a miserable one. I missed you each day and night.

AARON   You probably never thought of me. How goes the novel?

MARY   (*Sitting on the sofa*)   Nowhere. My hero keeps looking like you and my heroine seems to be like what I think I am. I have him telling the girl he loves her—but I'm not sure he does. Does he?

AARON   If you couldn't write a love story in Florence, you're a failure and should junk the project.

MARY   The question was—Does he love her?

AARON   (*Sitting beside her*)   He missed her excessively. He must love her.
(*They kiss*)

MARY   Isabel looked me over like a guard at Los Alamos. This is the first time I'll be in your home overnight. Does she disapprove?

AARON Undoubtedly.

MARY Do you?

AARON (*Teasing*) Well, the hotels are crowded and you can't go back to Washington so late at night—and I want to hear all about your travels—so—

MARY It's true, violent, untrammeled love—that's what it is, Aaron, darling! Don't feel guilty about me. I'm no child who's been ravaged by an old roué.

AARON (*Drily*) How graceful of you.

MARY Did I sound common?

AARON Only young. The fact is—you are. (*He rises and crosses to the bar*) It's tea time.

MARY Good! I'll have a Scotch and water. (*She sees the elaborate setup of glasses and bottles on the bar*) You're expecting a lot of company?
  (*She rises and goes to her purse on the library table*)

AARON (*With a nod as he mixes the drinks*) Preholiday guests. The family—and an audition for a writer my niece Jane has discovered in the Village. He does—if you please—jazz poetry.

MARY I can hardly wait.
  (*She takes out her compact and comb and checks her hair and makeup*)

AARON You'd better. Jane thinks you can open doors for him. She likes your work and is anxious to meet you. (MARY *nods*)

Before then—I have a visitor—a former co-worker of mine at Oak Ridge.

MARY I'll hide.
(*She replaces the comb and compact in her purse*)

AARON And later, a conference with John Devereaux.

MARY (*Crossing to him*) Well, I brought some reading with me.

AARON But—when all that's done—we go to dinner and talk—by ourselves.
(*He hands her a drink*)

MARY Here's to our time, alone. (*They drink*) On the way to your home I added up the time we've spent together.

AARON Mathematical survey of some kind?
(*They walk to the sofa*)

MARY More of a romantic one. Four months ago, Aaron Cornish was just a name and face I knew in print. (*She stares at him and sits on the sofa*) You know, most of your pictures are lousy. You should have new ones. (AARON, *smiling, nods*) And then, a dinner party and here I am—all dewy-eyed and short of breath. Why is that?

AARON You were once in love with your high school biology teacher and I look like him.
(*He drinks*)

MARY No. As a matter of fact, you remind me more of a collie dog I once had. (*He laughs*) He got distemper and they took

him away. I never got over it. (*She smiles*) Promise never to get distemper.
(ISABEL *comes out of* MARY's *bedroom and starts down-stairs.* AARON's *smile fades as he speaks to* MARY)

AARON   I'm interested in the results of your survey.

MARY   Well, with your side trips to all those secret places—and my side trips to those public places—we've only spent about two weeks together. Really together.

AARON   Which would sound more complimentary—"It seems like an hour" or "It seems like years"?
(ISABEL *crosses into the living room. She carries one of* MARY's *dresses*)

ISABEL   Excuse me. May I press this for you, Miss Macready?

MARY   Thank you, Isabel.
(ISABEL *moves into the hall*)

AARON   Oh, Isabel, none of us will be in tonight—so after drinks this afternoon—you're on your own.

ISABEL   Thank you.
(*She exits to the kitchen*)

MARY   Does she plan burning a hole in the dress?

AARON   (*Sitting beside her, his arm around her*)   I have the impression you've been approved. Say something soothing.

MARY   Butter on bread? Oil on water? Warm tea on a cool night? Cool tea on a warm night? How's that?

57

AARON Soothing.

> (*She leans her head on his shoulder. He rests his head on hers. They sit for a second, still and comfortable*)

MARY Dr. Cornish? Is there any chance you'll marry me? (*His smile fades; he lifts his head*) Not that it's required. Only that I love to be with you—care for you—look at you. (*He does not reply*) And if you tell me you're old enough to be my father, I'll scream. (*Still no reply*) Well, I'll even listen to that—just so you say something.

AARON I'm old enough to be your father. (*She draws away and looks at him, puzzled*) Oh, Mary, it would be no life for you. (*Rising and facing front*) And I suddenly feel cheap because this is no life for you.

> (MARY *rises and crosses to stand behind him, her cheek on his shoulder*)

MARY It's a beautiful life. You've given me tenderness I've never known. I want nothing else—except that you love no one but me the rest of your life.

AARON (*Turning to her*) That I promise.

CALEB (*Calling towards* AARON's *room as he comes down from the third floor*) Father?

AARON (*Moving a few steps*) Caleb, we're down here. (*As* CALEB *comes downstairs—proudly*) Caleb, this is Mary Macready!

CALEB (*Crossing to her*) Well, how do you do, Mary Macready! I've heard a great deal about you—all of it good.

MARY (*As they shake hands*) Thank you. Now I know where your father gets his good manners.

(CALEB *turns to* AARON *and they exchange a polite bow*)

CALEB Tell me, Father, when does Jane unveil her genius?

AARON They should be here in half an hour.

CALEB You know, since Amy found out—

AARON (*Interrupting*) Mary! I forgot to tell you. I'm going to be a grandfather!

MARY Oh, congratulations, Aaron! (*Remembering*) Ohhh, and you, too, Caleb.

CALEB It was nothing, really. Thanks, anyway. But—as I was saying—since Amy discovered she's with child, she is indulging herself—resting for two, she says—so I pamper her with tomato juice.

MARY Aaron tells me that your field is genetics.

CALEB Yes. Father and I are each concerned with a four-letter word. His—atom. Mine—gene. Both are receiving considerable attention these days.

MARY And they *are* related, aren't they?

CALEB In ways incalculable. But don't get me started. I'll give you nightmares. You're going to be with us for Thanksgiving —and that's fine. (*To* AARON *with a slight smile—knowing* AARON *and* MARY *want to be alone*) I suppose the kitchen would be a good place to find some tomato juice?

AARON Ideal.
> (CALEB *exits into the kitchen*)

MARY I give him high marks. Is he as smart as you?
> (*The door buzzer sounds*)

AARON I'd say he's smarter—I'm wiser.
> (*He goes to answer the door*)

MARY I remember. I'll hide.
> (*She gets her purse, hat, gloves and coat and comes back to the sofa as* AARON *opens the door to admit* BRONISLAUS PARTOS, *a man of about forty-five. He has a faint mid-European accent and is loquacious and restless*)

AARON Hello, Broni!

PARTOS Aaron! I enjoy seeing you.

AARON Let me take your coat.
> (*He helps* PARTOS *off with the coat and hangs it on the hall rack*)

PARTOS The years treat you well. Do you realize it's been four years since I've seen you?

AARON I do. You look well—and prosperous.

PARTOS (*As they move into the living room*) I am.

AARON Miss Macready—Mr. Partos. We worked together at Oak Ridge.

PARTOS (*Shaking hands with her*) A hundred years ago.
> (CALEB *enters from kitchen with a glass of tomato juice*)

MARY   How do you do.

PARTOS   Delighted.

AARON   Caleb! Look—

CALEB   Broni!
        (*He crosses to* PARTOS)

PARTOS   Caleb!

CALEB   How are you? Good to see you.

PARTOS (*As they shake hands*)   You look fantastic—almost well fed. You must be a full professor.

AARON   Why don't you sit with us, Caleb?

CALEB   I'd like to, but—
        (*He indicates the tomato juice*)

MARY   If you like, I can take that up to Amy.

CALEB   Fine. You'll know Amy. She's that divine creature in the third-floor bedroom. Tell her I miss her.

MARY   I will. Good-bye, Mr. Partos.
        (*She takes the glass from* CALEB *and starts out*)

PARTOS (*Hands extended after her*)   Beauty is what I search for and it always retreats from me.

MARY (*Smiling, turns briefly at the foot of the stairs*)   Thank you.

(She continues up the stairs, stopping to leave her coat, gloves, and purse in her room, then goes up to the third floor with the tomato juice)

AARON *(Pouring drinks)*   Broni, what have you been doing?

PARTOS   Making money—a good deal of it.

AARON   From the parking lot?

PARTOS   That's a thing of the dreary past. *(He pulls a check from his coat pocket)* I have here in my hand a check in full for the two thousand dollars you loaned me six years ago—with interest.

AARON   That isn't necessary, Broni.
         (He hands PARTOS a drink)

PARTOS   Of course it isn't. But when you loaned me the money —that was necessary to me. You are the only colleague who was generous and brave enough to help me.
         (He hands the check to AARON. CALEB, who has been listening with interest to this revelation, sits on the ottoman)

AARON   I knew you, that's all.
         (He sits down)

PARTOS *(In high good humor)*   Shall I tell you about your father, Caleb? He is a fool. *(He turns to AARON, who smiles)* I might have been a spy. Then where would you have been—disgraced—dishonored. *(He turns to CALEB)* Isn't that so?

CALEB   That's so.

AARON   Tell me, Broni (*He waves the check*) —is this all honest money?

PARTOS   Each copper penny. After I was branded and stamped and dismissed—I almost killed myself. (*He looks at* CALEB) This is true. I thought about it at great length. (*He thinks; then with a gesture of dismissal—*) Aah, but I prefer to stay alive and eat! So I come to Aaron and ask for help to buy a lease on a parking lot. (CALEB *looks quizzical*) I know—this is not a distinguished method of employment for an expert electronics engineer, but I had four children—all with enormous appetites and—*well*—one parking lot leads to another— then to a garage (*He sets his glass on the small table*) —all open—with beautiful ramps (*He indicates ramps*) and *soon* (*He takes a flower from the vase on the table and tucks it in his buttonhole*) —now I own four such garages and I have holidays in California and in New England and my children have each a garage in their name. And if they ask for a toy chemistry set (*He slaps his wrist*) —I slap their hands.

AARON   That certainly destroys the image of the starving innocent victim of security hysteria.

PARTOS (*Buttons his jacket*)   I am personally very grateful to the late senator. (*He bows solemnly*) He pushed me out of the stinking hot—or rather I should say antiseptic—air-conditioned laboratory into a fortune. I am a happy man.

CALEB   With no second thoughts, Broni?

PARTOS   Oh, many of them. Listen, Aaron—I think back to those days. Remember the fears? We feared the government. We feared the committees. We feared the investigators. We even feared each other. We were freaks to be guarded, examined, watched and carefully observed. Ha ha! And now—look at you—all of you. Ohhh, I am so amused. You are the new elite. Everyone now is afraid of you. You are the new tribal medicine man. To the rest of the world you speak a language to each other that only you understand (*Mysteriously*) —pimason—synchro clash—fluxes—gradients—quanta. Everyone now listens to you—the army and the Congress—and they fear you because of your secrets. Now, you listen to me, Aaron—be smart—don't tell them! (*They laugh*) I know you believe science must be free and open but, believe me, don't tell them. Keep them sitting on the hot seat. Ahhh, it is so wonderful and so funny to see the change. Now you say jump and they jump.

AARON Broni, my friend, no one tells Devereaux to jump.

PARTOS Ah, Devereaux. He can go jump in the lake. How is the old iceberg? (*Before* AARON *can reply,* PARTOS *picks up his glass and continues*) You know, Caleb, we used to say of Devereaux: He is an iceberg. (*He illustrates on his glass*) Seven-eighths of him hidden and all of it not worth looking at. Ha, ha! (*He drinks, then sits on the sofa and puts his glass down*) So—so—I am glad I am out of it. And you know why, Caleb. You well know. Because when I am an old, old man and my great-great-great-grandchildren come to me with their big ears and half-noses and four-toed legs—I will be able to say to them, I had nothing to do with the way you look—it was those other guys filled the air with strontium ninety. (*To* CALEB) Right? (*Rising—to* AARON, *who also rises*) Right?
(AARON *crosses to the bar for another drink*)

AARON Broni, you're driving me to drink.

64

PARTOS Aaron, my friend, it's a mad world. Get out of it and go into the garage business. Let us examine this ridiculous stupidity. You and I know that there will be no atomic war and the Russians know it. But it isn't war we should be afraid of. It's peace. A peace where they keep blowing up bombs to frighten each other and keep each other from making war. Boom! Tests in the air! Tests on the ground! Tests underground! And all the experts with their public quarrels: We can survive—we cannot survive. It's a clean bomb—it's a dirty bomb. There's a very serious hazard—ahhh, it's not so serious. And, meanwhile, we have peace—BOOM! (*His hands are high in the air to indicate the mushroom action of the bomb. Slowly he flutters his fingers downward*) Ahhh! A beautiful peace—with fallout and sickness and death. Ahhh (*He points a finger at* AARON) I say we are being deprived of a basic right. The right of each man to live or to die as he wishes.

AARON How many of us are given that luxury?

PARTOS That is the tragedy. Less and less of us each day. I go now. (*He shakes hands with* CALEB, *who rises from the ottoman*) I talk too much (*He turns to shake* AARON's *hand*) —and you, Aaron, not enough.
　　(*He starts out, but* AARON *stops him*)

AARON Broni—

PARTOS (*Turning*) Hmm?

AARON Do you miss the lab?

PARTOS That is a stupid question! What is there to miss? Does a bird miss his wings? Cage! I meant to say, "Does a bird miss its cage?" (*He pauses a moment*) Good-bye.

*(He darts out of the house, taking his coat from the rack
in passing)*

CALEB   Poor rich, sad Broni.

AARON   He's a good engineer. His brain would be of use.
(He drains his glass)

CALEB   Maybe he *is* using it, Father. Say, not that I'm counting,
but you've been belting down quite a few.

AARON   There's a chill in the air.

CALEB   When I spoke to Aunt Sue this morning, she asked me
to talk to you about the house. Well—what about the house?

AARON   Oh, she doesn't want me to sell it. Says I'd be parting
with tradition.

CALEB   Well, why do you want to sell it? Father, have you been
playing the horses?

AARON   *(Sitting in the chair near the sofa, with his fresh drink)*
Thinking about this trip I'm going to take, I thought I'd cut
down on everything.

CALEB   That makes sense. But when you get back, where are
you going to live?

AARON   I'd decide that when I got back—an apartment, perhaps.
Do you feel anything special about the place, Caleb?

CALEB   It's a wonderful house, but my roots are emotional rather
than material. You know I have little feeling about things.

When I do think about home, I think of you and Mother—
what little I remember of her.

AARON   What *do* you remember?

CALEB   Oh—first, I think of the day she was killed. Your coming
to school and getting me out of class and the gentle way in
which you told me—and when I saw her in the funeral parlor
—and my anger that her hair wasn't combed the way she liked
it. And the sound of her laugh. Oh, and her temper—(*He
smiles*) The way she used to say, "That's an old Spanish cus-
tom." And her eyes that always looked full; you could never
quite tell whether she had been laughing or crying.

AARON   It was such a sad, terrible, unnecessary death. An icy
street—a careless driver—and a life is gone. A life full of words
and dreams and hopes. Oh, I remember so very much.
      (*He gazes sadly down at the glass in his hand*)

CALEB   Father—suddenly as I look at you—I realize how lonely
you've been. There was little you could tell me at first—and
then I was in college and married. Now I feel there are things
you'd like to say, but you don't. Is there a time, Father—as you
grow older—when you can no longer say what you feel?

AARON   Do you mean—because we grow afraid—or because we
grow shy?

CALEB   I don't know. (*Crossing to stand behind* AARON) But just
a minute ago, I wanted to put my arms around you—like I did
when I was a boy—and say—"Father, I love you."
      (*Impulsively he puts a hand on* AARON's *shoulder.* MARY
      starts downstairs from the third floor)

67

MARY Caleb. (CALEB *moves into the arch, looking up*) Your wife *is* divine. We've decided she's to wear the red dress tonight and she misses you.

CALEB Thank you. She's spoiled. (MARY *enters her bedroom, closing the door behind her.* CALEB *turns back to* AARON, *who rises*) Mary's lovely. Obviously she adores you.

AARON (*Turning and moving a few steps*) Caleb, the stream of consciousness is a baffling thing. From your mother—to Mary—to the war—to this glass in my hand—to classrooms at Heidelberg—to Los Alamos—to Fred—lights flashing on an incredible switchboard, making old connections—severing new ones. A crazy house of fragmentary impressions of smells and colors—places and people— (*He hesitates*) You're quite right, Caleb. I have had a few!
    (*The door buzzer sounds.* CALEB *goes to answer*)

CALEB (*Opening the door to admit* SUSAN *and* FRED) Well! Look who's here!

FRED Hello, Caleb.

SUSAN (*Hugging* CALEB) Hello, Caleb, dear.
    (FRED *closes the door and hangs up his coat*)

CALEB Hello, Aunt Sue! It's good to see you!

SUSAN Where's Amy?

CALEB I'm just about to guide her down.

SUSAN (*Moving to hang up her coat*) Hurry her up. I'm dying to see her.

CALEB Well, Uncle Fred, you look wonderful!

FRED I feel lousy. More aches than I can count. When I tried to get up this morning—

CALEB (*Interrupting—escaping*) Yes, Uncle Fred—see you in a few minutes—
(*He goes upstairs*)

AARON You're both on time, as usual. Where's our distinguished guest?

FRED (*Crossing to the chair near the sofa*) The unwashed Longfellow ought to be here any second. Jane has to stop trying to be an impresario. (SUSAN *comes in*) I wish she'd settle down and get married—sometimes I don't care to whom —just get married.
(*He sits*)

AARON Will Buzz be here?

SUSAN He wasn't certain, Aaron. }
FRED I doubt it.   } (*Simultaneously*)

SUSAN (*Finishing lamely*) He'll try.

FRED Why lie about it? (SUSAN *spreads her hands in a gesture of resignation and sits*) We had a dilly this morning. I was having breakfast and he decided to have a man-to-man. I listened to him—and he kept rattling on as if he were talking to some customer.

AARON You listened—but did you hear?

FRED   He gave me the same old nonsense. Well, finally I told him—and told him good!

AARON   Fred!

FRED   I said I didn't want to listen to any more—

AARON   (*Cutting in*)   Fred—last night I defended you when Steven called you stupid, but he was right!

SUSAN   Aaron!

FRED   That's a hell of a thing—

AARON   (*Angry*)   That son of yours has been trying to get you to understand him ever since he got out of the Air Force. You've given him nothing but stuffy and stupid arguments. And one of these days, he'll get out of the house and tell you both to go to hell—

SUSAN   Aaron!

AARON   —and I for one won't blame him. (*A slight pause*) And if I hadn't had a drink just now, I never would have told you.

SUSAN   Well, I try to be patient—

AARON   Susan, you smother him and, Fred, you punish him. Let him alone! He's a man with a heart and a mind of his own.

FRED   I certainly didn't expect this from you.

AARON   What I resent is the loss of the life force—the waste of time! If we all knew we were going to die tomorrow, would we be so cocksure about everything we're doing? Would we be so positive—

SUSAN I've never heard you talk like this before!

AARON (*Continuing through her line*) —about what we believe? (*The door buzzer sounds*) Would we—? Aaaaah—I'll get it. (*Still angry, he crosses to the door.* SUSAN *moves to* FRED. AARON *opens the door to admit* LEIGH) Hello, Bob, and don't tell me liquor is bad for me. (*He starts up the stairs*) Come on upstairs.
    (LEIGH *removes his coat and hangs it on the rack*)

SUSAN (*Crossing into the hall*) Are you all right, Aaron?

AARON (*At the first landing*) Fine. Bob's buying some stock in a uranium mine. He wants my advice. When the other guests arrive, let me know.
    (MARY *starts down from her room*)

LEIGH (*As he starts upstairs after* AARON) Susan. Fred.

AARON Oh, Mary, you know Bob Leigh?

MARY Yes. Hello.

LEIGH Hello.

AARON You met my sister and her husband in Washington—

MARY (*She passes* LEIGH *and* AARON *and continues down*) Yes. How are you?

AARON You keep the party going, Mary. Bob and I have some matters to discuss.

(*He and* LEIGH *continue upstairs and into his room, closing the door*)

MARY (*Shaking hands*) It's good to see you again, Mrs. Ashe.

(FRED *rises and crosses into the hall*)

SUSAN Thank you. Is Aaron all right? I'm worried.

MARY He appears to be. (*To* FRED) Mr. Ashe, how are you?

FRED How do you do. (MARY *goes into the living room.* FRED, *who has been thinking of what* AARON *said, speaks quietly to* SUSAN) Do you think he could be right, Susan? Have I been that wrong?

SUSAN Fred, let's talk about it later. (*She crosses into the living room.* FRED *follows and goes to the bar*) Are you going to be here for Thanksgiving, Miss Macready?

MARY Yes. Aaron has asked me to stay.

SUSAN (*Not at all happy*) How very nice.

(*The lights dim down in the living room and come up in* AARON's *bedroom.* CALEB *and* AMY, *who started downstairs from the third floor as soon as* AARON *and* LEIGH *went into the bedroom and closed the door, reach the first floor. They move into the area of the living room, greeting and joining* FRED, SUSAN, *and* MARY *in silent pantomime*)

LEIGH (*As he and* AARON *are revealed in the bedroom*) Fred and Sue seemed in some state of shock.

AARON They were. We quarreled about Buzz. (*He paces*) The Scotch has loosened my tongue.

LEIGH I spoke to Dr. Fitzhugh again this morning. He wants me to go with you to Bethesda next week.

AARON All right. (*He puts down his drink*) Amy is going to have a child. (LEIGH *delightedly extends his hand to shake hands*) In seven months. (*A moment*) Boy or girl?

LEIGH Well, when I was doing O.B. work, I'd always tell the mother it would be a boy and I would write down on my chart that it was to be a girl. If it was a boy, they always remembered and, if it was a girl, I could show them the chart and tell them they forgot what I said.

AARON You told me I had six months—maybe longer. What did you write down, Bob?

LEIGH I didn't write anything. I don't know.

AARON I'd like to steal another month or two. I can't tell Caleb now.

LEIGH I understand. How do you feel?

AARON Why the language of your trade?

LEIGH Fitzhugh asked me to keep check. I'd like to examine you.

AARON (*As* LEIGH *makes a move to him*) I can read your mind?

LEIGH Yes?

AARON (*Unbuttoning his jacket and vest*) You're thinking—maybe they're wrong—all wrong—at Bethesda. Want to make a small bet?

LEIGH You know me. I hate to gamble. (*He places a hand on* AARON's *lower right rib area*) Breathe. Out.

AARON Bob—you'd be amazed how often people say life or death in ordinary speech—how lightly it is treated.

LEIGH (*He moves his hand on* AARON's *lower left rib area*) Breathe. Out.

AARON (*As* LEIGH *feels for the glands up and down* AARON's *neck, behind his ears and under the jaw*) I've been acutely aware of it these last few days—all my life—bet your life—till the day I die—not on your life—dead pigeon—dead duck—big as life (*He removes his glasses as* LEIGH *puts his on and examines the inside of the lower lid of each of* AARON's *eyes. As* LEIGH *finishes and they reverse the glasses business—*) —the rest of your life—*live with it.* (LEIGH *turns away*) Oh, Bob, I've been behaving stupidly. Why do I assume that, because I'm dying, I am suddenly blessed with some omnipotence—that I can hurl bolts of wisdom that will change people's characters and alter the course of their lives.

LEIGH The fact is, Aaron, we can do very little about changing anyone's character. All we can do is improve his manners.

AARON And how little we know about ourselves. I didn't know how lonely I was until Caleb told me five minutes ago. I need someone to listen to all that's coursing through my head. And when I feel that I'm about to burst with what I want to say,

74

it dams up again, making me choke. (*Attempting a joke*) What do I need—a sedative or another drink?

LEIGH I can get you either—or both.

AARON Do you have a prescription for courage?

LEIGH You'll find one. You're a smart man.

AARON Bob—if I ever let go, I'll become undone—like a skein of yarn.

LEIGH (*Extending his hands*) Can I help ravel?
(AARON *touches his hand in appreciation as the lights dim in the bedroom. As the lights come up in the living room,* FRED *sits in chair near the bar,* AMY *and* CALEB *sit on the sofa.* MARY *is standing near the bar and* SUSAN *is standing beside the picture of "The Highest Tree")*

SUSAN It's about forty years. My father had it painted for Mother. It's based on a German phrase she always quoted to us— (*She looks at* CALEB) Caleb, your German is better than mine.

CALEB *Wenn man auf einen Baum klettern will, dann klettert man auf den höchsten.*

SUSAN Thank you, Caleb. (*To* MARY) In English—"If you go tree climbing—climb the *highest* tree."

CALEB Precisely.

SUSAN Mother always said this to us. If we wanted to learn to skate—she wanted us to be the best. Always wanted us to aim high. Never settle for second best.

MARY (*Moving down to sit in the chair near the sofa*) Unfortunately, some of us must.

SUSAN (*Crossing to stand near* MARY) That's true. Mother never told us that the rest of us failed—but she always said that Aaron would climb the highest tree—and he has.

FRED (*Suddenly rising*) Susan—do you know Buzz's office number?

SUSAN Yes. Judson nine—four-two-two-one.

FRED Excuse me.
(*He goes into hall, takes the phone from its shelf and disappears into the library, closing the door behind him*)

SUSAN (*Her eyes going from* AMY *to* MARY) There is something very alike between you two. You could be sisters.

MARY (*Smiling—looking at* AMY) I'm complimented. But I'm much older.

AMY Also much prettier.

SUSAN Oh, Amy, you're adorable! Caleb's mother would have been so proud of you. (*To* MARY) Caleb looks very much like his mother. Caleb, how old would Carla have been?

CALEB (*A brief pause*) Fifty-one.

SUSAN (*Thoughtfully—looking at* MARY) Fifty-one. (MARY *is aware she is being reminded*) The years fly. Aaron's remained so lonely. It's easy to understand why. His romance with Carla was unique—especially romantic! They met in Paris in

nineteen thirty—a few months before Carla's family came to America. The Medinas were a very distinguished Spanish family, and their wedding was a beautiful one. Aaron and Carla were man and wife—but they always remained lovers.
(She pauses, feeling she has not only made her point but buried it into MARY. AMY *and* CALEB, *realizing what is going on, have exchanged a look.* MARY, *while listening, has already begun to frame her answer. She adjusts her position to sit squarely in the chair, leans forward with hands firmly planted on her knees)*

MARY   There's a story told of a man who once owned a beautiful gold shield studded with precious stones and engraved with exquisite patterns. The shield was stolen from him and he was sad. *(She looks at* AMY *and* CALEB) Many people loved him and brought shields to replace the one he had lost *(She looks at* SUSAN, *who turns away)* —but his *advisers* always rejected them. *(She looks front;* SUSAN *looks at her)* This one was silver—this one not precious enough *(Again to* SUSAN, *who looks away)* —this one not nearly as classic. No one ever asked *him,* so they didn't know he would have had some contentment from a shield not as precious as the gold one—but with some degree of protection.

SUSAN   *(Refusing to be aware)*   That's a lovely story. I never heard it before.

MARY   *(Looking at her)*   I just made it up.
(She rises and takes a cigarette from the small table. AMY *smiles at* CALEB, *who, smiling broadly, rises)*

CALEB   Well, we can have a drink on that, Mary Macready!
(The door buzzer sounds. SUSAN *escapes to answer it as*

77

CALEB *goes to the bar and* MARY *sits on the sofa, smoking her cigarette.* SUSAN *opens the door to admit her daughter* JANE, *who is gay and twenty, and* JANE'S *escort,* ARKADY CLARK, *a rather sullen but handsome young man. He carries a guitar case and wears a heavy sweater, tight trousers and has a car coat flung over one shoulder*)

SUSAN (*To* JANE) Hello, dear.

JANE Hello, Mother. This is Arkady Clark.

SUSAN How do you do.

ARKADY (*Hardly glancing at her*) Ma'am.
(FRED *has just emerged from the library*)

JANE Hello, Father.

FRED Hello, Jane.

JANE Arkady Clark, this is my father.
(*She starts into the living room*)

FRED (*Extending his hand*) Hello.

ARKADY (*Barely touching it with his left hand*) Hi.
(SUSAN *turns and looks upstairs thoughtfully.* FRED *places telephone on shelf—after closing the door to the vestibule —and then leans on column between the living room and hall, thinking deeply*)

AMY (*As* JANE *enters the living room*) Hello, Jane.

JANE Hello, Amy! Caleb!
(*She hugs him enthusiastically*)

78

CALEB (*Glass in one hand*) Jane, you're getting cuter by the minute.

JANE You both look marvelous! (ARKADY *has dropped his coat on the pouf. He now moves the vase of flowers to make room on the library table for his guitar case*) Arkady, this is my Cousin Caleb.

ARKADY Hi.

JANE His wife, Amy.

ARKADY Hi.

JANE (*Looking at* MARY) And—

CALEB Miss Macready.

ARKADY Hi.

MARY Likewise.

JANE Hello, Miss Macready. I've wanted to meet you for such a long time.

MARY Thank you.

JANE Where's Uncle Aaron.

CALEB (*Hands* AMY *the glass*) I'll get him.
        (*He exits upstairs.* ARKADY *opens the guitar case, takes out his guitar and tunes it through the following.* JANE *removes her coat and also places it on the pouf, looking at*

ARKADY *adoringly all the while.* FRED, *who has been standing deep in thought, moves to* SUSAN)

FRED Susan—I spoke to Buzz. He's meeting me at the house. Let's get out of here.

SUSAN Darling, we can't be rude.

FRED I knew he'd wear tight pants.
(*They move into the living room.* SUSAN *sits in the chair near the sofa and* FRED *sits in the chair below the bar*)

JANE (*To* MARY *and* AMY) Arkady doesn't want to stay too long. He hates conventional houses. Miss Macready, I think he has incredible talent. His stuff reads as good as it sounds!

MARY (*To* ARKADY, *as he tunes the guitar*) Have you written any fiction? (*Without looking at her, he shakes his head in apparent disgust*) Just poetry?

ARKADY Only my kind.

MARY Oh.
(*Meantime,* CALEB *has entered* AARON's *room, has shaken hands with* LEIGH, *and the three men have come downstairs—*AARON *first,* LEIGH *second, and* CALEB *last.* JANE *sees them and runs to meet* AARON *at the foot of the stairs*)

JANE (*Hugging him*) Uncle Aaron! Hello, Dr. Leigh. (*Turning to* ARKADY) My uncle, Dr. Aaron Cornish, and Dr. Leigh.

ARKADY Hi. Let's get the show on the road.

JANE (*Crossing to sit between* AMY *and* MARY *on the sofa*) Arkady's going to do only one of his poems.

80

(AARON *moves to the bar.* LEIGH *sits down.* ARKADY *turns his head slowly and stares at* AARON *until the latter pours himself a drink*)

ARKADY (*Looking about to see that everyone is settled*)   I don't want to be asked any questions about it. It is what it is. It's called—"Birth (*He strums*) Living (*He strums*) Death"— (*He strums. Now he talks his poem, plucking strings or strumming to fit the mood*)

"Birth is a slap, five fingers clamped into a paddle against the rump!
Then a shake—
After the groaning and the grunting and the sighing—
A loud *scream*—and then *crying!*
Crying for all that's to come. The pain of borning is like nothing to the pain of living.
So you greet life with a *scream!*
And you're born!
(*He breaks into jazz rhythm*)
"Man—you think you're way out—but you've had it.
You're in a world spinning at the rate of blank-blank-blank miles a minute
With blank-blank-blank millions of people
And, cat—you're there!
(*He stops the playing*)
"And the living takes over.
(*A new rhythm*)
"The living—Hell, that's groaning too—and screaming too.
It's full of the give-me-that's.
Give me a dream.
Give me a place.
Give me a gal, give me a stream and give me shoes.
Give me a car, give me a gun and give me food.

Give me a job, give me a son and give me gold.

Give me? Get it yourself.

Give me? Get lost.

Give me?

(*He beats a rhythm with his hand*)

"What do you want? Why do you yearn—strain—plead—pray
  —beg—hustle—plead—

Give you? *Drop dead!!*

(SUSAN *reacts*)

"That's living!

And death—dying—man, that's the end.

The ever living end!

And off you go and they write your name off the book.

You're off the hook.

It's the end!

(LEIGH *looks at* AARON. ARKADY *starts a new rhythm*)

"The inexorable, incandescent, irrefutable, irrevocable, excoriat-
  ing, excruciating—

In conclusion, End!

(*He stops playing.* AARON *looks at* LEIGH, *who looks down*)

"Paint the master stroke—a joke!

Write the blessed word—absurd!

Sing the highest C—not me!

Play the major chord—oh, Lord!

It's all gone—man—it's the end.

So long, my friend.

It's the end.

Light. Burn. Out."

(JANE *enthusiastically starts the applause. After a second,*
  FRED *exaggeratedly uncrosses his legs and slides down
  slightly in his chair*)

FRED   I haven't any questions.

Diana Douglas, Gloria Hoye, Robert Ritterbusch, and Elizabeth Cole, as MARY MACREADY, AMY CORNISH, ARKADY CLARK, and JANE ASHE

MARY I enjoyed that, Mr. Clark.

ARKADY (*Putting the guitar in its case*) You don't have to like it. Nobody has to like it.

SUSAN I found it quite exciting. You play the guitar wonderfully well.

JANE Would you do another, Arkady?

ARKADY (*Shaking his head and going for his coat*) I have to leave. I don't like crowded houses.

MARY Have you other poems I may read?

ARKADY (*Putting on his coat*) You wouldn't like them. They're all about death.

MARY Why?

ARKADY I'm afraid of it.
    (*He picks up the guitar case*)

AARON (*Casually*) Mr. Clark, have you ever faced death?

ARKADY Every day. (*A step toward* AARON) Don't we all? Good night, everybody.
    (*He goes into the hall*)

JANE (*Going for her coat*) I'll be with you in a minute, Arkady!
    (LEIGH *rises and helps her with her coat*)

ARKADY I'll wait outside.
    (*He goes out, closing the door*)

JANE Isn't he wonderful?

FRED Jane, he's a fraud. That's junk—plain junk.

JANE I think it has dynamics!

SUSAN He is impolite, dear.

JANE Thanks for your interest, Miss Macready.

MARY You're welcome.

JANE And thanks for the use of the hall, Uncle Aaron.

AARON A pleasure.

JANE (*Hurrying out*) See you all tomorrow!

SUSAN (*Rising*) Jane—I want you home early tonight.

JANE (*She knows* SUSAN) Ohhh, Mother! 'Bye!
(*She exits.* AARON *crosses to the hall*)

MARY What exactly does Jane do?

SUSAN She's an associate editor of *Seventeen*.

FRED (*Rising*) Nonsense! She just has a job there—learning the business. They asked her to find new talent merely to get her out of the office. Susan, we have to go. Good night, everyone.

SUSAN See you all tomorrow. One o'clock sharp.
(*She goes to the rack and puts on her coat as* FRED *moves to* AARON)

FRED   Believe it or not, Aaron—I not only listened, but I heard what you said.
(FRED *crosses up to* SUSAN *and they exit.* ISABEL *enters from the kitchen, carrying* MARY'S *dress on a hanger.* MARY *quickly rises and crosses to her*)

MARY   Thank you, Isabel.
(*She takes the dress and goes upstairs.* ISABEL *turns to* AARON)

ISABEL   Excuse me. Have you changed your plans, Dr. Cornish?

AARON   No, Isabel. (*He notes that she is wearing her hat and coat*) Are you going out on the town?

ISABEL   To church.

CALEB   Say a nice prayer for all of us.

ISABEL   I always do. Good night.
(*She goes into the kitchen*)

CALEB   (*Rising and crossing to place his glass on the bar*)   We ought to be on our way. Can we all dine together?
(AMY *rises*)

AARON   You forget. I'm expecting Devereaux.

CALEB   I did forget. (LEIGH *is near* AARON. CALEB *moves between them*) You two came from upstairs in a thoughtful mood.

AARON   Bob had a notion he discussed with me and I had the unhappy task of telling him that his high hopes were unfounded.
(*He crosses to the bar and pours another drink*)

85

LEIGH (*To* CALEB *and* AMY)   I can save you cab fare.

CALEB   Fine.

AMY   Thank you. Good night.
(*She and* CALEB *get their coats*)

LEIGH (*Calling up to the second-floor landing*)   Good night,
Miss Macready.

MARY (*Coming from her room to the railing*)   Good night,
Dr. Leigh. (LEIGH *goes to put on his coat*) I better change for
dinner. Isabel did such a fine job on the dress, I don't want it
to go to waste.

CALEB (*Looking up at her*)   See you here after the theatre.

MARY   Have a good time.

CALEB   How's your bridge game?

MARY   Lousy, but I'm great at slapjack.
(*She goes into her room, closing the door.* AMY *and* CALEB
move to the outer door)

AMY   Good night.

AARON   *Auf Wiedersehen.*

CALEB   *Auf Wiedersehen, herr doktor.*

AARON   *Leben Sie wohl!*

86

LEIGH (*As* AMY *and* CALEB *exit*) Be with you in a second. (*To* AARON, *looking at the drink*) Are you preparing for Devereaux? Or just enjoying yourself?

AARON In my running battles with Devereaux, I've always been at a disadvantage because we've both been cold sober.

LEIGH Tonight you may be stacking the deck against yourself.

AARON At Heidelberg, I had a Latin professor named Dr. Otto Schmidt. You could have a fever of a hundred and four and it made no difference to Herr Schmidt. You had to be perfect in your Lucretius.

LEIGH Well, I hope you get an A.

AARON That's the point. The only time I did, I went directly to his class from a beer hall.
  (*He drinks*)

LEIGH (*Smiles*) Good night.
  (*He goes*)

AARON (*He remembers a student song and begins to sing softly*)
"Ca, ca, geschmauset, lasst uns nicht rappelköpfisch sein!
Wer nicht mithauset, der bleib daheim.
Edite, bibite, collegiales
Post multa saecula-pocula nulla!
  (*He lifts his glass and increases the volume*)
"*Post multa saecula-pocula nulla!*
  (*He drains the glass and moves up to set it on the bar. Remembering* ARKADY'S *performance, he takes a stance near the library table and strums an imaginary guitar dramatically*)

87

"It's the end, my friend! The ever living end!"
> (*He dismisses this with a smile and a gesture and suddenly thinks of* MARY. *He crosses hall and starts upstairs as he calls—*)

Mary! Mary Macready!
> (MARY, *wearing a light robe and brushing her hair, steps out of her room*)

MARY Hello.

AARON (*Reaching her*) I don't care what Arkady Clark says. It's good to be alive.

MARY Yes, indeed.
> (AARON *embraces her hungrily. She responds, dropping the hair brush*)

Curtain

Scene 2

Scene: Some time later. It is dark outside. Only the living room lights are on. MARY's *bedroom door is closed.*

At rise: AARON *is at the bar pouring two drinks.* DEVEREAUX *appears in the vestibule.* AARON *picks up the two drinks and starts out of the living room as the door buzzer sounds. He glances up at* MARY's *door, is obviously annoyed by the interruption, and goes back to set the drinks on the bar. The door buzzer sounds again. He turns on the hall light and opens the door.* JOHN DEVEREAUX *enters. He is a powerful figure of a man. He projects authority and poise. His speech is deliberate and his eyes constantly on the move.*

DEVEREAUX   Good evening, Aaron.

AARON   Good evening, Devereaux. (AARON *closes the door and comes down to* DEVEREAUX) Are you well?

DEVEREAUX   I'm fine. How are you?

AARON   I'm fine—for the time being.

DEVEREAUX   (*Crossing into the living room.* AARON *follows*) Aaron, you must try to understand. My duty as head of a project has many uncomfortable moments and onerous responsibilities. We—you and I—have to face this situation together—as well as we can.

89

AARON I'll try. (*He goes up to the bar*) What'll it be?

DEVEREAUX Bourbon and water. Light.
(*While* AARON *mixes the drink,* DEVEREAUX *removes his coat and places it over the back of the chair near the sofa*)

AARON It occurs to me belatedly that I should have had dinner for you.

DEVEREAUX Thank you, but I'm having a late dinner with Rogan. I hope this hour hasn't complicated your dinner plans.

AARON It hasn't.
(*He hands* DEVEREAUX *his drink*)

DEVEREAUX (*Lifting his glass automatically*) Good luck.

AARON (*Ironically*) Cheers.
(DEVEREAUX *realizes his toast was a gaff, but decides not to comment*)

DEVEREAUX Spoke to Fitzhugh. He said he had your permission to give me the diagnosis. He also told me you're going to Bethesda next week with your own physician. (AARON *nods*) Perhaps there may have been some miscalculation.

AARON No. Devereaux, let's spare me the guarded word. It's acute leukemia. We both know what that means. We both saw it happen to Margoti.

DEVEREAUX A man could learn something from his courage. (AARON *crosses to the sofa*) He was incredible. Worked until the last week.

AARON I don't think I'll be able to. (*Turning*) You knew Margoti better than I did. What kept him during those last months so preoccupied with his work—fear of death or devotion to his task?

DEVEREAUX Margoti's was a private world few of us ever entered. He approached each meal, each drink, a game of cribbage or a problem in the same two-fisted concentrated fashion. Get it done. Finish it. That probably accounted for his bad stomach and his gambling losses.
(*He drinks*)

AARON So—your guess is he was neither afraid nor devoted. Just *obsessed*.

DEVEREAUX (*Gives him a sharp look*) That may be.
(*He sits in the chair near the sofa*)

AARON What about Schlorsberg? How did he go?

DEVEREAUX That wasn't the same.

AARON I know. It was cancer. But what about him? I was in Japan during those months.

DEVEREAUX He was afraid. He ran to religion—not out of conviction, but out of naked fear.

AARON How would you know that?

DEVEREAUX I knew Schlorsberg for sixteen years. I never heard him use the word "God"—except in a curse.

AARON   Many deeply religious people seldom use the name of God.

DEVEREAUX   I was reporting an observation, not making a judgment.

AARON   Perhaps Schlorsberg wasn't afraid. Perhaps he was filled with sudden hope.

DEVEREAUX   (*Anxious not to argue*)   That's possible, of course. I must say, he died peacefully.

AARON   (*Moving down to* DEVEREAUX's *left*)   I wonder about myself. That's the real question in these circumstances. What aspect will you take—what attitude will you hold?

DEVEREAUX   We will do whatever you ask of us.

AARON   Is there something special you can do?

DEVEREAUX   (*Setting his glass down*)   Well, perhaps all we can do is listen. Among us—I don't mean us personally, but as a group—there is a special trust—a special language and, indeed, and most important—a special responsibility—that is shared by members of our community of interest. I remember army men speaking of this odd fraternity of emotions. It's a particular identity because of the experience of going through a common adventure and bearing a common obligation.

AARON   An elite. That's what Broni Partos said we had become. He was here this afternoon.

DEVEREAUX   How is Broni?

AARON   Seemed fine.

DEVEREAUX   Good man—but a clown.

AARON   But hardly a traitor.

DEVEREAUX   He was never called that.

AARON   But the implication was—he had the makings.

DEVEREAUX (*Angry*)   It wasn't my charge.

AARON   You made no effort to defend him!

DEVEREAUX   There was a clear and present danger!

AARON   But not created by Broni! (*A pause as he regains control*) It's history. But Broni's no clown. Canaveral would be a count down ahead with him.
  (*He finishes his drink and goes to the bar for a refill*)

DEVEREAUX (*Picking up his glass*)   Aaron—
  (*He watches* AARON *pour a generous portion into his glass*)

AARON   Yes? (DEVEREAUX *searches for the right words*) Go ahead.
  (AARON *drinks Scotch throughout the following scene and becomes quite drunk as it progresses*)

DEVEREAUX (*Crisply*)   Aaron, in the next few weeks you'll have to give some thought to some of the men who have been working with you. Those best equipped and able. Those to whom you can pass on your notes—your thoughts.

AARON That will be done. I said, "*That* will be done"—not "*Thy* will be done."

DEVEREAUX (*Controlling his exasperation, he crosses to set his glass on the small table*) What about Prager?

AARON Able. But not as able as Proxmire or Manning.

DEVEREAUX Either one of them or both suits me.

AARON No—there's another—better than all of them. Lonnie Walker. He has the free mind.

DEVEREAUX Free? Or undisciplined?

AARON The best mind. He'll give you the most trouble but, also, the most satisfactory results.

DEVEREAUX It's your decision to make, Aaron.

AARON Thank you. Walker it is. I'll see him in Washington next week. Won't take too long. He's *au courant* with most of my work.

DEVEREAUX (*Picks up his glass*) It would be of great value, Aaron, if you also took time to write out some of your experiences and observations.

AARON Biographical, philosophical, sociological, or scientific?

DEVEREAUX I'd say a bit of each. Any or all of it would be important for the journals.

AARON (*Indicating the liquor*) Want one, Devereaux?

DEVEREAUX (*Pulling back his glass*) No, thanks. (*He watches* AARON *pour another stiff drink. He sets his own glass on the small table and reaches for his coat*) We can continue another time, Aaron. I've kept you too long.

AARON (*Moving down to block him*) I'm not hungry. Feel like talking. I've often wondered. We all call you "Devereaux." Why don't we ever call you by your first name?

DEVEREAUX You may if you wish. John.

AARON (*Thinking it over*) I prefer Devereaux. (*He crosses and sits on the arm of the sofa*) Now then. You want me to set down my feelings. What I believe—what I've done—what I stand for. (*Lashing out*) Make up a satchel of words and say, "Here it is, and inside is Aaron Cornish."

DEVEREAUX Not a satchel to be put away somewhere unopened, but—rather—a vessel from which we can pour all that you know. A vessel that represents a fine mind and how it worked and what it accomplished.

AARON Where would it begin? The day I was born? I have no recollection of the event.

DEVEREAUX Obviously I'm provoking you without meaning to. I regret that.

AARON (*Almost to himself*) You've been provoking me for years.

DEVEREAUX We find it difficult to talk to each other—always have. I had no idea you dislike me so intensely.

95

AARON I don't. I'm indulging myself with liquor and some re-flections. Shall I tell you something, Devereaux? (DEVEREAUX *does not answer. Obviously, he would like to leave but, out of consideration, does not*) I will. This is what we all should have been doing for the last fifty years—hundred years!—thousand years!—learn to talk to each other. The Europeans to the Asians—the Asians to the Africans—the Americans to the Europeans—talk to each other—quietly. But all we do is scream at each other—frighten and maim and kill each other.

DEVEREAUX Perhaps—

AARON (*Rising and crossing*) Oh, don't patronize me! Don't be kind to the noble warrior as he breathes his last.

DEVEREAUX Aaron, I came here to perform a most unhappy assignment. I didn't come here to quarrel with you.

AARON No. You've been decent. Glacial—clinical—but decent. So extraordinarily decent. (*Angrily*) But I've got six months, Devereaux! You can wait a while before you pick my suc-cessor—set down my last words. I need no guarantee of lavish mention in the scientific literature for me to finish my job.

DEVEREAUX Perhaps I do not merit your appreciation, but I don't believe I deserve your contempt.

AARON I'm sorry. None of us say "I'm sorry" enough times. Tell me, Devereaux, am I haunted or mad when I say that we— all of us (*He waves his hand between them*)—should say "we're sorry"? We're sorry we built a bomb and started an age—a new age of terror and destruction—on the flesh of the people who lived in Hiroshima and Nagasaki!

DEVEREAUX T.N.T. bombs did as complete a job—in Coventry —or Hamburg. People died just as permanently.

AARON But this was one bomb. One beautifully conceived and magnificently engineered bomb. One bomb that represented an amalgam of the finest minds in a triumph over matter.

DEVEREAUX When history is being made, the makers cannot judge it. If I had built the bomb myself and if I were to die now—I could not say I was sorry. If I live to be a hundred— I would have no reason for saying it.

AARON Bully for you.
 (*He moves somewhat uncertainly toward the mantel as* DEVEREAUX *takes his coat from the chair*)

DEVEREAUX In your own memoirs you are, of course, free to think or say whatever you wish to think or say.

AARON A fifth freedom—from top secret.

DEVEREAUX (*Throwing his coat over back of the chair—finally furious*) Don't place me in the role of a monster, Aaron! There was a war and it had to be won! And war, regrettably, cannot concern itself with irresolution. With the war over, we dreamed of peace, didn't we? This new age need not be an age of bombs—but that's not our unilateral decision—we have an enemy to face! We are only doing what circumstances dictate must be done.

AARON Indeed we are.

DEVEREAUX (*Moving two steps toward* AARON) What do you propose, Aaron? Tell the Russians we're sorry and weary? You win? We're tired?

AARON I propose nothing!

DEVEREAUX Aha!

AARON But I've been looking back and I have questions. Questions about the age of the big explosions that we've designed—whether our names are Russian or English or American.

DEVEREAUX Big explosions have leveled mountains, Aaron—built dams—changed the face of the earth. Science creates something in the hope that it will serve man. If man perverts it—subverts it—should science abdicate? Do we turn the clock back? Destroy all modern artifacts—throw the cyclotrons and piles and isotopes and all the paraphernalia of the last century into the Grand Canyon, cover it with dust and proclaim, "It's done! (*He raises his hands, palms out*) Man is now saved!" If man is stupid enough to want to kill, he will create new weapons—or scrape the dust off the old ones.

AARON (*Crossing to* DEVEREAUX) Now, Devereaux—you don't really believe all man is stupid—just all the others—away from us few bright ones.

DEVEREAUX Who are those others you believe I'm slandering? Which ones? Which ones, Aaron? The ones who puncture each other with knives and bullets? The ones who rape, murder and rob? The ones who talk of fidelity and commit adultery? Science has given man twenty-five extra years of life—and that extra time has been used only for fornication.

(AARON *turns away*) Don't resort to "*mea culpas*," Aaron, just because you're facing—(*He stops himself.* AARON *turns*) You've merely had too much to drink.

AARON (*Furious*) If someone scratches you, Devereaux—what comes off? Skin—or stainless steel?

DEVEREAUX (*Taking his coat*) I'm leaving, Aaron. Indignation never persuades me.

AARON (*Letting go with passion born out of drunkenness*) I am indignant! Goddam indignant! I'm indignant with this malignancy that eats at my body. I'm indignant at the cold implacable logic that takes us so logically, step by step, to disaster. I'm indignant with all the lies—the hundreds of lies we all tell. That the Russians tell. Listen to me, Devereaux! It's all piled up inside of me here—like sick vomit! Why not tell the truth about how the air and the sea and the earth is being poisoned—of the places where man can no longer live? Why not! Then the fears would come bubbling up—and out of it would come a wave—a tide of indignation that would flood the politicians and diplomats and generals—yes, and the scientists—out to a sea of reason and drown them—all of them! (*He weaves drunkenly, then pats his lips with his hand*) Sorry. Speak no evil.

DEVEREAUX Why you have berated me, I do not know. (*He crosses to the door*) I'm neither your doctor nor your executioner.

(*He exits, slamming the door. As the door slams,* MARY *comes out of her room, leaving the door open. She is unseen by* AARON)

99

AARON (*Shouting*) Good night, Devereaux!! (*Weaving, he turns back, looks down at the glass in his hand and, in sudden revulsion, smashes it into fireplace. He is very ill and weak. He stumbles a few steps. He extends his arms at his sides and in frightened agony screams—*)CARLA! (*He stumbles another step and falls to his knees, his head in his arms on the floor, sobbing wildly.* MARY *reaches him at this moment, sinking to her knees, trying to lift him up. He wraps his arms about her and she holds him*) Darling—darling. I need you. I need you. Oh, Carla—Carla—my love. I'm so frightened—so terribly frightened. Help me, Carla. Hold me—hold me.

Curtain

ACT THREE

Scene 1

Scene: It is later that night.

At rise: AARON *is in his bed, sleeping quietly.* DR. LEIGH, *who stands beside the bed, unscrews a syringe, stores it in his black bag, takes* AARON's *pulse, picks up the black bag and crosses to the door. He glances back at the quiet figure, turns out the light and leaves the room, closing the door behind him.*

Meanwhile, MARY *is discovered in the living room. Once she thinks she hears a sound from upstairs and looks toward the stairs. Then she goes back to the window. As she hears* LEIGH *on the stairs, she crosses and meets him just inside the living room.*

LEIGH (*Putting his black bag on a chair*) He's resting.

MARY Can I get you anything?

LEIGH No, thanks. He ought to sleep until morning. (*He looks at his watch*) I'll wait a few minutes to make sure, then I'll run along.
    (*They walk toward the center of the room*)

MARY He's really all right? (LEIGH *nods*) If I hadn't been able to reach you, I don't know what I'd have done. I was terrified.

LEIGH He merely had too much to drink and his stomach rebelled. He's not accustomed to more than a highball or two.

MARY That's all?

LEIGH That's all. (MARY *sits in the chair near sofa, troubled*) If he's at all uncomfortable during the night, let me know.

MARY I will.

LEIGH (*Taking out his cigarettes*) You just returned from Italy, didn't you?

MARY Yes. (*He offers her a cigarette*) No, thanks.

LEIGH (*Lights one for himself*) I haven't been there since the war. I saw most of it—but it wasn't really sightseeing. I liked Florence. (*He crosses to the mantel*) I spent a weekend there. I had the feeling that to see it one needs a year.

MARY Dr. Leigh, before Aaron became ill, I held him in my arms. Devereaux had gone and he had crashed a glass into the fireplace there. Then he collapsed. (LEIGH *nods*) He spoke to me—not knowing it was me. In his poor unhappy state he thought he was talking to his wife, Carla.

LEIGH Well, he was drunk.

MARY (*Rising*) I know. I love Aaron with all my heart. Today I asked him to marry me. He was kind—and evasive. (*Breaking*) His sister, Susan, would rather I'd disappear into the East River.

LEIGH (*Moving a few steps to her*) Miss Macready, you're desperately tired and off guard—

104

MARY (*Crossing to him—speaking firmly now*) I'm not tired and I'm deliberately telling you all this for a reason. Please listen.

LEIGH Miss Macready, Aaron has never given me confidence regarding his affection for you—but I do know he's been working extremely hard. That and the liquor might have—

MARY What, Doctor?

LEIGH I don't know really. If you're asking me for advice, I can't help you.

MARY I'm not, Doctor. I'm asking for something else.

LEIGH What?

MARY (*Still watching him intently*) What's wrong with Aaron?

LEIGH Alcoholic inflammatory gastritis (*He escapes her gaze for a second by putting out his cigarette*)—translation: He had several too many.

MARY Doctor, I know he's dying.

LEIGH (*Determined to put her off*) Not tonight, he isn't. He did appear quite ill, but he'll be fine in the morning.

MARY I admire your poise, Doctor, but it isn't going to work. I know he's dying—because he told me so.

LEIGH (*Momentarily off balance*) When—what did he tell you?

MARY He was frightened. Talking to Carla, his wife, he told her that he had six months to live. What's he dying of?

LEIGH People articulate many fears when they're drunk. It's absurd. He's not dying.

MARY (*Looking away for the first time*) I'll ask him in the morning.

LEIGH Why are you pursuing this?

MARY (*Looking at him*) Because I love him. I'm not going to leave him. I'll stay with him here or any place he wants me to stay. If he wants to call me Carla or any other name. (*She begins to break*) I only know that he's alone—and he needs someone—all of someone—every minute and every hour and every day. And I want to be here, if it's for six months or six years—if only to hold his hand. (*She is crying*) Tell me! Please, Doctor! I won't tell anyone. Not him or anyone. (*She controls her crying*) Is it cancer?

LEIGH No. (*He looks at her for a moment, then steps toward her*) God forgive me, I'm going to tell you—because I trust you. It's acute leukemia. (MARY *bows her head*) He's told no one. I know. Devereaux knows. That's all.

MARY (*Quietly*) He said six months. Is that all?

LEIGH Just about—for a man of his age.

MARY What can I do?

LEIGH Love him. As the time goes—I'll tell you. There are some things that we will try and do—blood transfusions—perhaps

bone-marrow transfusions. None of these things will cure. Perhaps they can delay. (*Her control goes. She sinks into the chair, sobbing*) Mary—if you're not strong enough—I've done a dreadful thing in telling you!
(*She controls her sobs, rises, and looks at him*)

MARY I'm strong enough.

LEIGH Next week I'm taking him to Bethesda. You'll be in Washington—
(AMY *and* CALEB *have entered the vestibule and, at this point, burst into the hall*)

LEIGH Hello.

AMY Hello—

CALEB Well—look who's here.

MARY How was the show?
(AMY, *who is crossing into the living room—still wearing her coat—opens her mouth to answer but* CALEB *beats her to it*)

CALEB (*Taking off and hanging up his coat*) Tremendous! Beautiful sets! Beautiful music! Beautiful girls!

AMY (*Sitting on the sofa*) *Exactly* the kind of show for a young, intelligent geneticist!
(*She slips off her shoes*)

CALEB Where's Father?

LEIGH Your father got himself stoned and is in his bed sleeping it off.

CALEB (*Crossing to the sofa*)   Oh, no.

AMY   Is he ill?

LEIGH (*As* MARY *sits down again*)   Just blotto. Mary and I man-
aged to get him upstairs as he spoke eloquently in German,
some Spanish and what sounded like Latin—and with a sedative to calm his stomach, he's sound asleep.

CALEB (*To* MARY)   I knew he was way above his quota. The
evening's turned out to be a fine washout for you, Mary.

MARY (*Smiling*)   Not at all. Dr. Leigh is good company.

AMY   Maybe the news that he's to be a grandfather threw him
into a state of shock. (LEIGH *laughs, goes for his coat and puts
it on*) You know the first thing my father said when we told
him, "Imagine my daughter doing such a dreadful thing to
me!"
      (CALEB *crosses to* LEIGH)

LEIGH   Well, see you all tomorrow.

MARY (*Simply*)   Thank you, Doctor.
      (*She rises, moves up to the library table, lights a cigarette
      and listens*)

LEIGH (*Picking up his black bag*)   He'll sleep well, I'm sure.

CALEB   Bob, none of this sounds like Father. Is there anything
wrong with him?

LEIGH   Nothing that I know of. (*He decides to be more con-
vincing*) I know he's been tired—probably had a few drinks

108

to pep himself up. Ohhh—and he had a *long* session with Devereaux which may have increased his interest in drinking.

CALEB That could be. What'll we do with his head in the morning?

LEIGH Treat it gently. 'Night.

CALEB Good night. (LEIGH *exits.* CALEB *locks the door and turns out the vestibule light*) Anybody for a cold drink? *Soft!* (*He returns to the living room*)

MARY (*Putting out her cigarette*) No, thanks. I'm tired. Do you mind if I pass up the slapjack?

CALEB Certainly.

AMY (*Looking at the stairs as she picks up her shoes and rises*) If I don't go up now, I'll never make it later. I'm exhausted.

CALEB (*Intercepting her at the end of the sofa*) Run along, Amy. (*He kisses her gently*) That'll hold you until the next time we meet.

AMY Good night, Mary.
   (*She starts upstairs and continues to the third floor*)

MARY Good night, Amy. Good night, Caleb.
   (*She crosses into the hall*)

CALEB (*Turning off the living room light*) Mary, Father's going to be very apologetic tomorrow.

MARY (*Stopping at the foot of the stairs, looking front*) He needn't be. He was a perfect gentleman.

CALEB (*Coming down to her*) This is new for him.

MARY I know.

CALEB I don't know what started him off on this blast—but, whatever it was, he'll forget about it in the morning.

MARY I'm sure of it.

CALEB Luckily he has the constitution of a rhinoceros.

MARY (*For the first time, she looks at him and then away*) Yes, that is lucky. (*She looks at him again*) Good night, Caleb. (*She starts upstairs*)

Curtain

Scene 2

Scene: It is the following day—Thanksgiving—almost noon. It is a clear day and the sun streams through the windows. The autumn leaves in the vase below the painting have been replaced by a huge bouquet of giant chrysanthemums.

At rise: DEVEREAUX *is in the living room. He looks at his watch and then gazes at the painting. His coat is on the sofa.* AARON *enters from the kitchen. He is dressed and, apparently, suffers no bad effects from his illness of last night. He walks directly into the living room.*

DEVEREAUX   Good morning, Aaron.

AARON   Good morning, Devereaux. First, my apologies for last night.

DEVEREAUX   I had determined to forget that.

AARON   Please don't. I meant all I said—excluding the personal references to you.

DEVEREAUX   I, also, made some intemperate remarks.

AARON   Thank you for coming here this morning (CALEB *starts down from the third floor with a breakfast tray*)—but it is important. And let me assure you that today I'm neither angry nor drunk.

DEVEREAUX   I'm aware of that. I have to go south; otherwise, I'd have canceled my plane reservation.

AARON   I won't keep you long.

CALEB (*Reaching the foot of the stairs*)   Good morning, Father.

AARON   Good morning, Caleb.

CALEB   Hello, Mr. Devereaux.

DEVEREAUX   How are you, Caleb? How's your work going?

CALEB (*Moving just inside the living room*)   Fine, thank you.

AARON   If you'll get rid of that tray, Caleb, I'd like you to sit in with us. If you don't mind, Devereaux?

DEVEREAUX   Not at all.

CALEB (*Seeing no place to put the tray*)   I'll be right back.
        (*He exits through the kitchen door, closing it behind him*)

AARON   He doesn't know about my illness and I don't want him to know as yet. He just learned he's going to be a father.

DEVEREAUX   I understand. Last night I had neither the grace nor the opportunity to tell you how damned sorry I am—
        (*He stops as* CALEB *returns*)

AARON   Caleb, I've made a decision to quit my job and I wanted you here when I spoke to Mr. Devereaux about it.

CALEB (*Wanting to ask a question, but deciding against it*) Yes, Father.

DEVEREAUX (*Surprised*) Quit! Now?

AARON In two weeks—enough time to brief Walker or anyone else you select.

DEVEREAUX Well—this is, as you might have guessed, a surprise.

AARON I imagine it is to you, too, Caleb.

CALEB (*Sitting on the ottoman*) Quite a surprise!

DEVEREAUX Why have you decided to do this?

AARON For many reasons. Mainly because, thinking about last night, I realized that my conflicts with you, Devereaux, are based on the fact that for years I've worn a muzzle on my tongue—and on my conscience.

DEVEREAUX You've always had the gift—and the freedom—of saying whatever you wished.

AARON Not in public. Two nights ago my son asked me for permission to join a committee to fight resumption of bomb testing. Because of that muzzle I was conditioned to say to him I'd think about it. Then, when I heard he was to be a father, I went halfway and told him to join. Now I want to go the rest of the way. I plan to join with him and use my voice and my mind as forcefully as I can.

DEVEREAUX Aaron, after all your years of work for the government, anything you say will be misinterpreted or misconstrued.

AARON (*Sitting in the chair near the sofa*)   Possibly.

DEVEREAUX   In these times there are some things we must accept. We must learn, as the saying goes, "to live with it."

AARON   Yes—if we grow old—or bald—or become sick—or suffer defeat. But if we can effect any change, then it's a sin to "live with it."

DEVEREAUX   Last night, I asked you what you proposed. You said you could propose nothing. Have you suddenly found an answer?

AARON   I only know that your answer won't work, Devereaux. (*Rising*) The policy of defending a nation with a plan for mass extermination is suicide—also immoral—also there is no chance for delayed admission of error.

DEVEREAUX   Aaron, in my mind I've gone through all the risks and possible dangers. Stripping away the imponderables, my position is simply this: I would rather be dead than live in a slave world.

AARON   So would I. But do we have the right to make a private decision that can affect the lives of millions of people and the existence of future generations? And are you certain that the only alternative to submission is death?

DEVEREAUX   Our only alternative to keeping our freedom is to surrender it.

AARON   I don't think so. Another alternative may be *more* freedom. More freedom for more people through political orders, balances and concepts never tested nor even conceived.

DEVEREAUX   It seems to me, Aaron, if a bear is pursuing you, you climb the nearest tree. You play safe and concern yourself later with the future. (*He looks at* CALEB) Wouldn't you agree, Caleb?

CALEB   It occurs to me, sir, you might not have much of a future if the bear can climb as well as you can.

AARON   When I came in, Devereaux, I saw you looking at that painting. It reflects an ambition of my mother—that one day man would climb the highest tree of accomplishment.

DEVEREAUX   That's a lofty ambition.

AARON   Yes, it is. And I wonder—in building this atomic world, have we climbed the highest tree, or merely *your* nearest tree?

DEVEREAUX   (*Taking his coat from the sofa*)   It's an age-old question. For me, the scientist, in political terms, must remain an arm of defense—not a philosopher.

CALEB   (*Rising and crossing to* DEVEREAUX)   May I say something, sir?

DEVEREAUX   I'm sure you disagree.

CALEB   I do. In Russia—as in America—children are being sickened by strontium ninety. I don't think the Russians want to die any more than we do. The fight against strontium ninety *is* in the domain of the scientist. As he builds atomic power, he fights against it and—since he finds himself wearing two hats—can he *help* becoming a philosopher? Is it moral to plan destruction and immoral to think of tranquillity?

115

DEVEREAUX I respect your concern for the future, Caleb. Your father has told me that your wife is going to have a child. My congratulations.

CALEB Thank you.

DEVEREAUX (*Crossing to* AARON) Obviously, you will not reconsider.

AARON No. I plan to spend my time working with my son. (*They shake hands*) I'll be in Washington Monday morning. We can work out a statement of resignation at that time.

DEVEREAUX Good-bye, Aaron, and Happy Thanksgiving. (*He turns to* CALEB) Good luck, Caleb.
    (*They shake hands*)

CALEB Thank you, sir.

DEVEREAUX Aaron, do you really think man can change his nature?

AARON I think that if man can split the atom and fly into space, he can—with time—do anything.

DEVEREAUX That's a sentimental thought, Aaron. I hope he has enough time. (*He walks to the door*) I'll see you Monday.

AARON (*Following*) Good day, Devereaux.

DEVEREAUX (*As he goes out*) Good day.
    (AARON *closes the door and turns back.* CALEB *joins him—excitedly*)

CALEB Father, did your getting drunk lead to this decision or did this decision lead to your getting drunk?

AARON It's hard to tell where one left off and the other began.

CALEB How much time are you planning to give to this?

AARON All I've got.

CALEB That's wonderful, Father! This is going to be a rather important newspaper item.

AARON I suppose it will.

CALEB Welcome to the ranks. (*A brief pause*) We need you! I've got to tell Amy. She'll be delighted. (*Starts, then turns*) When are you going to tell the rest of the family?

AARON At dinner today. (*The door buzzer sounds.* CALEB *hesitates*) Go on up. I'll take it.
   (CALEB *goes up the stairs to the third floor as* AARON *opens the door, admitting* LEIGH)

LEIGH Good morning, Aaron.

AARON Good morning, Bob.

LEIGH (*Removing and hanging up his coat*) What's the morning-after like?

AARON (*Moving downstage*) It's extraordinary. No signs of a hangover. There are actually signs of an appetite.

LEIGH (*Following* AARON) You can get away with one of those —I hardly recommend it as a nightly pick-me-up.

AARON I know. Actually, liquor is no comfort to me. My brain feels as though it has wandered about indecently exposed.

LEIGH You were fairly comatose when I got here.

AARON Obviously Mary must have called you. (LEIGH *nods*) Were Caleb and Amy here at the time?

LEIGH No; you were safely tucked in bed when they came home.

AARON It must have been a miserable experience for Mary.

LEIGH I've seen registered nurses do worse.

AARON Did she say anything?

LEIGH Nothing immortal.

AARON I mean—did I say anything to her while I was—*non compos mentis?*

LEIGH No, not that I know of. Haven't you talked to her this morning?

AARON No. She isn't here.

LEIGH Oh?

AARON I didn't get up till quite late and by that time she'd gone.

LEIGH   You mean she's gone? Left?

AARON   No. Isabel told me she had an early breakfast and went out.

LEIGH   Well, it's a nice day and she probably felt like taking a walk. I wouldn't worry about her. She's sophisticated and strong-willed.

AARON   You're sure she said nothing to you that might be of— well—that I ought to know?

LEIGH   Nothing—except that she loves you. You knew that, didn't you?
   (*The door buzzer sounds.* AARON *anxiously crosses to open the door, admitting* SUSAN *and* FRED)

AARON   Happy holiday!

SUSAN   Aaron, dear, I came early to check everything with Isabel.
   (FRED *takes her coat from her shoulders and hangs it on the rack and removes and hangs up his own*)

AARON   You will be discreet?

SUSAN   Of course. (*She goes into the living room to place her purse on the secretary.* AARON *follows*) Good morning, Bob.

LEIGH   Good morning, Susan.

SUSAN   It's a heavenly day, isn't it? Aaron, Reverend Martin's sermon today was about Thanksgiving and the Atomic Age. (*He looks at her*) It was brilliant.

FRED (*Moving just inside the living room, as he rubs his back*)
Brilliant's an extravagant word. I must admit that for a few
minutes he made me forget the pew was so damn uncomfortable. (*To* LEIGH) How are you, you old pill pusher?

LEIGH Me, I'm fine. But I'll bet you're not.

FRED I'm glad you're here, Bob.

LEIGH Why? What's wrong?

FRED I'm in absolute agony.

SUSAN Oh, Aaron, we'll only be twelve at dinner after all. Jane's
friend, Mr. Clark, has declined.

AARON Regrettable.

FRED (*Settling into a chair with difficulty*) Frankly, it was me
or him.

AARON What's your affliction this day?

FRED Oh, it's my back.

SUSAN (*Patting his head lightly*) It's purely psychosomatic.
Quarrel with Jane—backache.
(*She exits into the kitchen as* CALEB *starts down from the
third floor*)

FRED (*Calling after her*) We live in a world where everyone
practices medicine. (*To the others*) Susan is Chancellor
Emeritus. You know, there are no people as vain as the

William Prince, Howard St. John, Kenneth MacKenna, Natalie Schafer, and Richard Anderson, as DR. ROBERT LEIGH, FREDERICK ASHE, AARON CORNISH, SUSAN ASHE, and CALEB CORNISH

healthy. They besiege you with panaceas, doctors' phone numbers, mysterious ointments and advice—oceans of advice.

LEIGH   In medical school we were told we *all* have bad backs because we got off our front paws and walked up straight.

FRED   Maybe so, but it's too damn late to get back down.

CALEB   (*Entering*) Good morning! Good morning! Happy Thanksgiving, Fred!

LEIGH   Hello—

FRED   Caleb.

CALEB   How is everybody today?

AARON   Fred has a backache.

FRED   And I'd be pleased to discuss it!

CALEB   Poor Uncle Fred.

FRED   None of you believe this, but actually I'm no hypochondriac. That's true, isn't it, Caleb?
        (AARON *walks to a window and looks out*)

CALEB   You've got my vote, Fred!

LEIGH   Not mine.

FRED   So now you're going to tell me this backache is psychosomatic?

LEIGH Could be.

FRED Well, I've sure been keeping you in the upper brackets by my imaginary diseases. There's been tonsillitis, appendicitis, sinusitis—

LEIGH Diverticulitis—

FRED (*Rising*) Diverticulitis, neuritis, dermatitis—and a mess of other itisises. Then measles, mumps, pneumonia, the flu, viruses of twenty species—the herniated disc—and cracked ribs—then those gallstones—and *that kidney* stone! All make-believe, huh? (LEIGH *shrugs*) Well, the next time you send me a bill, I'll tell you you just *imagined* I was in your office!

STEVEN (*Flinging open the hall door*) The Steven Cornishes! (*With him is* GLORIA, *his wife, a youngish woman, too made up, too well dressed*)

AARON (*Quickly moving to greet them*) Welcome, Gloria.

GLORIA (*Kissing him*) Hello, Aaron. Happy Thanksgiving. (*As they entered,* STEVEN *took* GLORIA'*s coat from her shoulders and hung it up.* AARON *now takes* STEVEN'*s coat and hat and hangs them up so* STEVEN *can follow* GLORIA)

FRED Happy Thanksgiving, Steven—Gloria.

STEVEN Same to you.

GLORIA Hello, Fred.

STEVEN Caleb! Happy Thanksgiving!

SUSAN (*Entering from the kitchen*) Happy Thanksgiving, everybody!
(*She stands near* FRED)

GLORIA *and* STEVEN Happy Thanksgiving.

SUSAN Gloria, you look wonderful! That's a beautiful dress!

AMY (*Coming down from the third floor*) I had a late breakfast—but I'm ready for an early dinner.

CALEB (*Extending a hand toward the second-floor landing*) That's my girl said that!

STEVEN Hello, Amy—and congratulations! I heard the good news.

AMY (*From the stairs*) Thank you.

CALEB I had something to do with this (*The door buzzer sounds*) —and I'd like some of those congratulations! !

FRED Okay, let's give him a hand.
(*They applaud.* ISABEL *has opened the front door to admit* JANE *and* FREDERICK, JR.)

JANE Hello, Isabel! Hi, Uncle Aaron!

FREDERICK, JR. Happy Thanksgiving, Isabel! Uncle Aaron!
(JANE *spins into the living room, kissing her mother, greeting* CALEB *and the others and, finally, standing by* FRED, *who puts his arm about her.* FREDERICK, JR., *greets* SUSAN *and is excited to see* CALEB. *He and* CALEB *stand talking animatedly*)

STEVEN   Hello, Bob.

LEIGH   Hello, Steven—Gloria.

AMY   How are you, Uncle Steven?

STEVEN   Fine.

GLORIA   You look marvelous, Amy. I'm glad to see you.

AMY   This is getting to be quite a large family.

STEVEN   You're doing your best to make it a larger one.
(*The door buzzer sounds again.* AARON, *who has been waiting anxiously, opens the door, admitting* MARY. *She wears a dress with a sports coat over it*)

AARON   Good morning, Mary.

MARY   Hello, Aaron. I'm sorry that I'm late.
(*The conversation in the living room has continued through this*)

GLORIA   When's the baby due?

AMY   June—we think.

FRED   Perfect month for babies! That's when I was born.
(*The family now see* MARY *and greet her*)

FRED   Hello, Mary Macready!

JANE (*Taking* FREDERICK, JR., *by the arm*)   Buzz, I want you to meet Miss Macready. (*They go to her in the hall*) Miss Macready, this is my brother, Buzz.

124

MARY How do you do.
(They shake hands)

FREDERICK, JR. How do you do.
*(JANE and FREDERICK, JR., move back into the living room
as STEVEN and GLORIA arrive in the hall to be introduced)*

AARON Mary, I don't believe you've met my brother, Steven
Cornish, and his wife, Gloria.

GLORIA *(As they shake hands)* Delighted to meet you.

STEVEN *(Shaking hands)* How do you do, Miss Macready.
Charmed.

MARY *(Obviously somewhat overwhelmed by the picture of the
entire Cornish family together)* Please forgive me. I'll only
be a minute or two. I'll freshen up. Don't wait dinner for me.
I'll join you in a minute.
(She starts upstairs)

STEVEN Take your time, Miss Macready. We've some drinking
to do.

AARON *(Who is still by the stairs)* Isabel, please start serving
drinks in the library. Susan.
(ISABEL crosses into the library)

SUSAN This way, everybody.

FRED I'm ready.
(He starts slowly)

STEVEN Come along, Gloria dear. I'm thirsty.

GLORIA You usually are.
  (*They move toward the library door*)

FREDERICK, JR. A little champagne today—courtesy of the Steven Cornish Enterprises!

STEVEN I can't make money on this family!

JANE (*Stopping in the hall*) I wish Arkady were here. He has a wonderful poem about Thanksgiving.

FRED I'll be glad to hear it—*next* Thanksgiving.

AMY (*She and* CALEB *have been standing near the sofa, talking. Now they cross*) I'm warning you all—I'm eating for two!

CALEB I'm drinking for three!
  (*They exit into the library*)

FREDERICK, JR. (*His arm about* FRED's *shoulders as they go into the library*) How's your back, Dad?

LEIGH (*Following them*) He'll deaden the pain with some liquor.

FRED (*Off*) It's better than your prescriptions.
  (SUSAN *closes the door behind them and turns to* AARON, *who has moved just inside the living room*)

SUSAN Aaron, why aren't you coming with us?

AARON I'll wait for Mary and then be with you.

SUSAN Aaron, please don't be long. This *is* family day.

126

AARON Please, Susan. (*She goes into the library. Sounds of the happy din within are heard as she opens the door and closes it.* MARY *comes downstairs*) I'd like to talk to you, Mary. (*He indicates the living room and she crosses toward him*)

MARY I'm sorry if I delayed dinner. I lost track of time.

AARON Perfectly all right. Since I cheated you out of dinner last night, you're probably quite hungry.

MARY No. I made up for it with a good breakfast. I was up early and I felt like getting out for a while. How do you feel?

AARON Fine. I want to apologize for my bad behavior last night.

MARY I have an Uncle Mike who used to really tie one on every night, so the experience wasn't a new one for me.

AARON Regarding the events of Wednesday night last: You have indicated to the court that you witnessed all that took place.

MARY (*Accepting the improvisation*) No, sir. Not all. The first thing I heard was a door slam—and then somebody yelled, "Good night, Devereaux."

AARON (*With a faint groan*) Of course. I remember most of it—until Devereaux walked out. Complete your lurid testimony.

MARY (*Sitting in the chair*) You mumbled—threw a glass into the fireplace—and promptly went to sleep. After a while, you took ill. I called Dr. Leigh. He got you upstairs and into bed and that was that.

127

AARON Did I ramble on about anything?

MARY A few disconnected thoughts—

AARON About what? I'm interested.

MARY Well, none of it made much sense really. (*She smiles*) Embarrassing, isn't it?

AARON Quite. I've always thought of myself as a sensible man.

MARY Oh, not at all. You talked about Heidelberg. Said you wanted another drink. Talked about Thanksgiving being a family holiday and—as I said—mumbled.

AARON But—nothing—top secret?

MARY You did say something about two-R-squared equals Y plus Z—I think.

AARON Fascinating. (*He turns away*) Mary, I'm going to Washington Monday morning.

MARY (*Rising and crossing to him*) So am I. Isn't that a coincidence?

AARON (*Turning to face her*) What's a pretty, young, talented girl like you doing with an old professor like Aaron Cornish?

MARY (*She eyes him for a moment*) I'm trying to improve my mind.

AARON No—seriously.

MARY Seriously—I love you.

AARON What if I turn out to be fickle? After some months you're liable to find yourself fresh out of dates.

MARY (*Turning and moving away*) Then I'll have good memories of six wonderful months.
(*Too late, she realizes*)

AARON (*Coming up behind her—hands on her arms—gently*) How do you know it will be six?

MARY You said some. Now some, to me, always means six. Whenever anyone asks me to have some candy, I take six pieces. . . . (*She turns to face him, trying to laugh*) I'm a pig. (*She becomes serious—determined*) You're not sending me away, Aaron. I'm the most stubborn person you ever met.

AARON Yes, you are.

MARY Aaron, dear, no more questions. I know and you know that I know (*Her composure is going*) —and I intend to be with you tomorrow—and the day after—and the day after that—

AARON No more questions. (*He holds out his arms and she moves into his embrace, weeping quietly. He holds her a second, then looks down at her*) Mary, in science we not only have a count down which is a contraction of time, but we have a count up which is an expansion of time. So six months is one hundred eighty days—or four thousand, three hundred twenty hours—or—and this is the tough one—two hundred fifty-nine thousand, two hundred minutes. That's a big mass of minutes and I have a great deal to do. Will you help me?

MARY *(Smiling)* With each minute.
(He puts his arm about her and they walk toward the library)

Curtain